Early Perry County, Mississippi Newspapers
{Births, Deaths, and Marriages}

by Robert J. McSwain, Jr.
& Allison R. McSwain

Other Books by Robert J. McSwain, Jr.:

Descendants of Early Settlers of
Perry County, Mississippi

The Blue & The Grey,
Perry County, Mississippi's Civil War Soldiers

Military History of Perry County, Mississippi,
American Revolution to World War II

The McDonald Family
{Descendants of Angus McDonald}

The McSwain Family
{Descendants of Donald McSwain}

Cover Photo: Robert J. McSwain, Jr.

In Memory of
Robert J. and Kathleen McSwain,
loving parents & grandparents

Acknowledgements

My father and I would first and foremost like to thank our Lord and Savior, Jesus Christ, for His constant provision and grace. Thank you also to Judi McSwain, a very supportive wife and mother. We are extremely grateful to the University of Southern Mississippi for keeping such an extensive collection of historical records and allowing us to conduct research for this book in the Cook Library. Finally, thank you to you, reader, for expressing interest in what we have compiled. May you enjoy what you find here.

Allison R. McSwain

Table of Contents

Introduction

Perry County, Mississippi was formed from the western half of Greene County, Mississippi on February 3, 1820, and was named after Commodore Oliver Hazard Perry, a popular naval hero of the War of 1812. It was the first county formed after Mississippi attained its statehood in 1817, and the sixteenth county to be formed out of the old Mississippi Territory. The first settlement in Perry County was Augusta, founded in 1812 on the banks of the Leaf River. Augusta would become the county seat, and in 1819 was one of the first land offices in the state to be established. By 1860, two more communities, Enon and Monroe, had been established. It wasn't until 1882 that Hattiesburg would be founded by pioneer lumberman and civil engineer, William H. Hardy. Shortly afterwards, Perry County's first newspaper, the *Hattiesburg Herald* would begin publication on Saturday with C. L. Adamson as the editor. Other newspapers soon followed in the *Herald's* footsteps. The *Hattiesburg Democrat* (1885) began publishing every Saturday, the *Hattiesburg Progress* (1885) was published on Tuesday and Friday, and the *Courier* (1887) was published on Thursday. In 1888, the *Hattiesburg Day Book Gazette* began publishing on Saturday followed by the *American Citizen* (1892) which published on Friday, and the *Saturday Evening Eye* (1904), which published on Saturday.

In 1902, Augusta relocated across the Leaf River, to be near the new Mobile, Jackson, & Kansas City railroad, and changed its name to New Augusta. In April 1906, by an act of the Mississippi State Legislature, Perry County was divided in half, with the western part becoming the newly formed Forrest County, Mississippi (named after Confederate General Nathan Bedford Forrest). This left Perry County without any newspapers until 1906 when *The Richton Dispatch* began its weekly publication under the direction of Dr. Willis Walley in Richton, Mississippi. The newspaper was sold to L. A. Wilson, Sr. in 1914 and continues to be published by his grandson Larry Wilson to this day. In 1912, editor and publisher Eugene Terry started publishing *The Perry County News* as a weekly newspaper in New Augusta, Mississippi. However, it ended its publication in 1924. This book is a compilation of the birth, death, and marriage announcements of the citizens in Perry County from those early newspapers that have been preserved on microfilm.

Births, Deaths, and Marriages

1900 - 1910

The sudden and unexpected death last night of Mr. John F. Champenois, which event occurred about 8 o'clock, has greatly shocked this community and occasioned much sorrow. Mr. Champenois had been complaining of slight indisposition for several days, but his aliment was not deemed at all serious, and the announcement of his death from heart failure came as a great surprise. Mr. Champenois was one of our most progressive and broadminded citizens and his death will be deeply deplored by business acquaintances as well as an extensive circle of personal friends. He leaves a wife and large family to mourn their loss, and in their grief they have the sympathy of hundreds of our citizens. The absent members of the family have been notified, and the funeral services will take place at the family residence this afternoon at 4 o'clock under the auspices of Hattiesburg Commandery, Knights Templar. Interment at City Cemetery. *The American Citizen,* February 15, 1900, Vol. VIII, No. 20

The honorable Mayor Hall, of this city was married last night to Miss Elvira Wiley, at the home of the bride's sister, Mrs. Hartzog, in Silver Creek, Lawrence County, the Rev. Mr. Williams officiating. The wedding was a quiet affair, only close friends of the contracting parties and relatives, being present. Mr. Hall and bride will return to Hattiesburg today and make this city their home. The Citizen, together with friends of the bride and groom, extend most hearty congratulations. *The American Citizen,* February 15, 1900, Vol. VIII, No. 20

This evening at 8:30 o'clock, at the residence of the bride's parents, Mr. and Mrs. W. F. Roberts, Mr. Edgar B. Parker will lead to the altar Miss Eula Montressa Roberts. The many friends of the contracting parties extend congratulations.
The American Citizen, February 15, 1900, Vol. VIII, No. 20

Cards are out announcing the approaching wedding of Miss Louise Pace and Mr. Wake Bates, which happy event will occur next Thursday evening, Feb. 22.
The American Citizen, February 15, 1900, Vol. VIII, No. 20

Married: At McLaurin, May 25, W. E. Daniels and Miss Alberta Martin; Bro. Ellis of Brooklyn, performing the ceremony. The happy couple will leave this week for their future home, Beaumont, on the Mobile, Jackson and Kansas City railroad.
Hattiesburg Dailey Progress, May 27, 1902, Vol. III, No. 151

Mr. and Mrs. Walter Maddock's baby, Walter Windham, died this afternoon.
Hattiesburg Dailey Progress, June 17, 1902, Vol. III, No. 169

Charles W. Phillips, who is with Hawkins & Co., wholesale, left yesterday afternoon for New Orleans where he will tomorrow be married to Miss Lily Gray of that city. H. L. Foote accompanied him and will be best man.
Hattiesburg Dailey Progress, June 17, 1902, Vol. III, No. 169

The Progress deeply sympathizes with Mr. and Mrs. Walter Maddox in the death of their baby, Walter Windham. The funeral took place this morning from the family residence and was conducted by Rev. I. P. Trotter. *Hattiesburg Dailey Progress*, June 18, 1902, Vol. III, No. 170

Chas. W. Phillips, of this city, and Miss Lily Gray, of New Orleans, were united in marriage yesterday afternoon. Mr. and Mrs. Phillips will spend a few days on the coast before coming to this city. They have the congratulations of a host of friends.
Hattiesburg Dailey Progress, June 19, 1902, Vol. III, No. 171

Rev. S. J. McBride, living on River Street and who came to this city some time ago from Copiah County, died this morning. He was a Christian gentleman and a good citizen.
Hattiesburg Dailey Progress, June 23, 1902, Vol. III, No. 174

Mrs. McNair, wife of W. M. McNair, died at home in this city Saturday night after an illness of about ten days. Her remains were interred this morning in the Hickory Grove cemetery. The Progress tenders Mr. McNair its deepest sympathy in his great bereavement.
Hattiesburg Dailey Progress, June 23, 1902, Vol. III, No. 174

There was a little romantic marriage at the Commercial hotel yesterday, the ceremony being performed by Judge Robertson. The parties of the first part are Rupert Rhodes and Miss Dora Bailey, both of Lux up on the Gulf and Ship Island railroad. It was not a Gretna Green affair, but the parties concluded that it would be just as convenient and cost but little more to come to Hattiesburg and have the knot tied, being aware that a marriage knot tied by a judge generally remained until death us do part. *Hattiesburg Dailey Progress*, June 23, 1902, Vol. III, No. 174

There was a marriage at the Courthouse at an early hour this evening, the parties being Thomas Beech and Mrs. Patsey Shaws, Justice E. J. Wall performing the ceremony in his shorthand style. The parties are of middle age and live in the eastern part of the county.
Hattiesburg Dailey Progress, June 25, 1902, Vol. III, No. 176

Ed B. Davis is "tickled to death: over the arrival of a fine 8-pound boy at his home this morning. Mr. Davis proposes to "open a keg of nails" and invite all his friends.
Hattiesburg Dailey Progress, June 26, 1902, Vol. III, No. 177

Married- T. J. Castanera to Miss Margaret Frentz at 9 o'clock yesterday morning at Scranton. The ceremony was performed by Father Ten Brink. The bride and groom will arrive in Hattiesburg this afternoon. Mr. Castanera is manager of the local telephone company and his many friends join us in congratulations.
Hattiesburg Dailey Progress, June 26, 1902, Vol. III, No. 177

Lee Sartin, step-son of Dr. E. J. Mitchell, died this morning at 1 o'clock and was buried in the city cemetery this afternoon. Lee had been sick for six months and was a great sufferer. He bore the pain with great fortitude and expressed a perfect willingness to go. He was a splendid boy just reaching manhood's estate and the Progress deeply sympathizes with the bereaved family in his death. *Hattiesburg Dailey Progress*, June 28, 1902, Vol. III, No. 179

Belle Pearce, daughter of J. C. Pearce, living a few miles from Augusta, died Saturday morning and the remains were buried in the family graveyard yesterday, Rev. E. J. Currie of this city conducting the ceremonies. *Hattiesburg Dailey Progress*, July 1, 1902, Vol. III, No. 181

The remains of J. G. Foster were laid to rest yesterday evening in the city cemetery. Owing to the heavy rain falling at the time the attendance was small.
Hattiesburg Dailey Progress, July 10, 1902, Vol. III, No. 189

Fred Beiner, who came to this country from Switzerland several years ago, died at his residence Saturday night and was buried yesterday. He arrived in New Orleans from his native country where he married, when he re-moved to this city and followed his profession of paper hanging and painting. It is supposed that he died of paralysis, as he once before had a stroke of that disease, but of late years his health had gradually been declining and he had become discouraged, so much so that he was heard to say that he would prefer death if he knew that he had no chance to get well. He made a good citizen and was generally well liked by those who knew him. *Hattiesburg Dailey Progress*, July 14, 1902, Vol. III, No. 192

Annette, the little daughter of Dr. and Mrs. C. M. Hyde died last night. They have the sympathy of many friends in their bereavement.
Hattiesburg Dailey Progress, July 17, 1902, Vol. III, No. 195

Miss Lula Davis died yesterday at Rawls Springs after a few days illness. She was the daughter of Rev. Mr. Davis and was deservedly popular wherever known.
Hattiesburg Dailey Progress, July 14, 1902, Vol. III, No. 192

Married in the city of Hattiesburg on August 7, 1902, J. B. Hensarling and Miss J. C. Coleman, Rev. E. J. Curry officiating. *Hattiesburg Dailey Progress*, August 8, 1902, Vol. III, No. 214

T. O. Sewall, the cleaver foreman of the Phoenix Steam Laundry, is rejoicing over the arrival of a fine girl at his home last night.
Hattiesburg Dailey Progress, August 11, 1902, Vol. III, No. 216

The little child of Oscar Carroll died yesterday evening after a few days' illness. *Hattiesburg Dailey Progress*, August 21, 1902, Vol. III, No. 225

W. E. Martin is the happiest man in Hattiesburg. A fine girl has arrived at his home. *Hattiesburg Dailey Progress*, August 26, 1902, Vol. III, No. 229

The eight months old child of Mr. Graham, who lives on Newman Street, died yesterday and was buried in the city cemetery today.
Hattiesburg Dailey Progress, August 28, 1902, Vol. III, No. 231

Married at the home of the bride's brother in Hattiesburg, August 28, H. L. J. Barrus and Miss Mary E. Hauenstein. Rev. E. J. Currie officiating.
Hattiesburg Dailey Progress, August 29, 1902, Vol. III, No. 232

Mr. H. L. J. Barnes and Miss Mary Hauenstein were married last night at the home of the bride's brother, R. C. Hauenstein, of this city. Mr. Barnes is a member of the Macon, Miss., bar and is well known in Hattiesburg. Miss Hauenstein has visited her brothers here on several occasions and has a number of friends in this city. Only members of her brother's families were present, the affair being very quiet on account of the recent death of the bride's brother. Rev. E. J. Currie officiated. *Hattiesburg Dailey Progress*, August 29, 1902, Vol. III, No. 232

The Progress is a little late, but it is "better late than never" in congratulating Mr. F. W. Foote over the arrival of F. W. Jr., a few days ago. Our best wishes are for the new ruler of the household. *Hattiesburg Dailey Progress*, September 3, 1902, Vol. III, No. 236

On September 3, E. C. Cook of Hattiesburg and Miss Willie Z. Sigler of Waynesboro were united in the holy bonds of matrimony. They are at the residence of O. J. Bowen and are receiving the congratulations of many friends.
Hattiesburg Dailey Progress, September 5, 1902, Vol. III, No. 238

The Progress sincerely regrets to record the death of little Frankie Dean, the 18 days old daughter of Mr. and Mrs. W. M. Conner. The death of the little one occurred yesterday morning and she was buried yesterday afternoon. This was the first daughter of the household and naturally the fond parents are deeply grieved that her little life so soon be ended and their bright hopes so soon crushed. But the Master knows best and called the little one to himself. May God comfort and sustain the sorrowing parents.
Hattiesburg Dailey Progress, September 8, 1902, Vol. III, No. 240

Married at the home of the bride in this city this morning, T. E. Martin and Miss Faustena Milner. Rev. E. J. Currie officiating. The Progress congratulates the happy couple and wishes for them the greatest of happiness and prosperity.
Hattiesburg Dailey Progress, September 11, 1902, Vol. III, No. 243

The friends of Mr. and Mrs. E. P. Magee deeply sympathize with them in the death of their little son, William Prentiss. The funeral services were conducted this morning at the family residence by Rev. Louis Gates, and the body was interred in the city cemetery.
Hattiesburg Dailey Progress, September 13, 1902, Vol. III, No. 245

Mrs. Ella Moore, wife of W. L. Moore, died yesterday afternoon at the residence of John M. Powe after an illness of several weeks. Her remains were carried to Forest, her old home, for interment. She was a good woman, highly esteemed by all who knew her.
Hattiesburg Dailey Progress, September 17, 1902, Vol. III, No. 248

Today at the Main Street Methodist Church Miss Lula Travis Hawkins and Rev. William Burwell Jones were united in the holy bonds of wedlock, the bride's brother, Rev. W. L. Hawkins, of Brookhaven officiating. The ceremony was beautifully performed and the church was handsomely and artistically decorated. The presents were numerous and costly. Mrs. Heidlberg was matron of honor, R. R. Swittenberg was best man and Miss Alice Bass of Enterprise, maid of honor. The ushers were W. H. Cook of this city and H. L. Risher of Lumberton.

Just before the arrival of the bridal couple a double quartette rendered a beautiful wedding chorus, and during the ceremony the low sweet strains of "Annie Laurie" were rendered by Mrs. N. H. Howell on the organ, accompanied by her daughter, Miss Alma, on the violin. After the ceremony a reception was held at the home of the bride's mother, Mrs. M. E. Hawkins and an elaborate and toothsome repast was served. Miss Hawkins that was, is one of Hattiesburg's most popular young ladies and is endowed with all the sweet and noble graces that tend to make the perfect woman. Rev. Mr. Jones is a rising young Minister of the M. E. Church and is now located at Escatawba. The happy couple leave this evening for a bridal tour and carry with them the best wishes of a host of friends.
Hattiesburg Dailey Progress, September 18, 1902, Vol. III, No. 249

In the death of W. A. Bounds which occurred last night Hattiesburg loses one of her best and oldest citizens. Mr. Bounds had been sick some time and his death was not unexpected to his family and friends. He was a mason, confederate veteran and a good citizen. His remains will be carried to Jasper County tomorrow and interred with masonic ceremonies.
Hattiesburg Dailey Progress, September 19, 1902, Vol. III, No. 250

Married at the Court Street Methodist Church last night, Mr. W. A. Bilbo and Miss Lizzie Johnson, both of this city, Rev. W. M. Sullivan officiating. Attendants- Sims Bilbo and Miss Albertina Johnson. Ushers- A. M. Jackson and G. P. Smith. The church was beautifully decorated and crowded to its utmost capacity. Miss Bertha Olson of Canton presided at the organ and under her skillful touch the music was entrancingly sweet and appropriate. The bridal couple were the recipients of many beautiful presents. After the ceremony an elegant reception was greatly enjoyed by the invited guests at the home of D. S. Hall. Mr. Bilbo is a splendid young man and is highly esteemed by all who know him. His fair bride is the daughter of Mr. T. B. Johnson, a well-known attorney of this city and is a young lady of accomplishments and beauty. The Progress congratulates the happy couple and extends its best wishes for a bright and happy future. *Hattiesburg Dailey Progress*, September 19, 1902, Vol. III, No. 250

Mrs. R. A. Jones, who lived near Newman's Chapel died last night. Her remains were interred in the McInnis Cemetery at 4:20 this afternoon.
Hattiesburg Dailey Progress, September 22, 1902, Vol. III, No. 252

Miss Cleo Pool and Prof. Everett Butler were united in marriage last night at the home of the bride, Revs. W. H. Huntley and E. J. Currie officiating. The attendants were Henderson Pool and Miss Jessie Allen. The bride is one of Hattiesburg's most lovable young ladies and the bridegroom is a well-known and popular educator. They have the best wishes of the Progress for a happy future. *Hattiesburg Dailey Progress*, October 1, 1902, Vol. III, No. 260

The home of Mr. Guyton on 4th Street was the scene of a very pretty wedding Sunday afternoon. At 3 o'clock Rev. I. P. Trotter made Mr. J. E. Graham and Miss Pearl Guyton husband and wife. The marriage was somewhat of surprise to most people. Special friends were present on the occasion-a comfortable room full of them. The parlor in which the marriage ceremony took place was neatly decorated. Later the company were invited to the supper table which was loaded with good things of many kinds.

The weather was auspicious-an ideal October day. May the sun ever beam brightly on their married life. *Hattiesburg Dailey Progress*, November 10, 1902, Vol. III, No. 294

E. R. Cook and Miss Mattie Woods were married today by Rev. I. P. Trotter, and left on the 12:20 train for Monroe, La., their future home.
Hattiesburg Dailey Progress, November 11, 1902, Vol. III, No. 295

It was Polk instead of Cook who married Miss Mattie Woods yesterday. The notice was sent to the Progress by some friend who made the mistake.
Hattiesburg Dailey Progress, November 12, 1902, Vol. III, No. 296

At the residence of Rev. E. J. Currie today between 11 and 12 o'clock J. P. Jarvis and Miss Mary Dunham were made husband and wife, Rev. E. J. Currie performing the ceremony.
Hattiesburg Dailey Progress, November 12, 1902, Vol. III, No. 296

Victor A. Shoemaker and Miss Mabel M. Eure were married yesterday afternoon at 5 o'clock by Rev. I. P. Trotter at the home of the bride's father on West Fourth Street. They left on the 7 o'clock train for their future home, Monroe, La.
Hattiesburg Dailey Progress, November 28, 1902, Vol. IV, No. 1

There was a quiet marriage at the beautiful residence of Capt. T. J. George last night, the parties being Virgil Jones and Miss Carrie P. George, Rev. E. J. Currie performing the ceremony. These are well known people of the city, having lived here for quite a number of years, and very popular. Miss Carrie is the daughter of Capt. T. J. George, one of the most successful businessmen of the city, and is one of the most popular young ladies of this city. Virgil Jones, who has been in business in the city for a number of years, not only building up himself in the commercial world, but among his fellowmen in all south Mississippi, is a fine specimen of Mississippi manhood, courteous; gentle and one of our most progressive citizens. The Progress joins the many friends of this couple in wishing them a long and happy life.
Hattiesburg Dailey Progress, December 5, 1902, Vol. IV, No. 7

There was a boy baby born to Mr. and Mrs. W. E. Thrash last night about 9 o'clock. It tipped the scales at nearly twelve pounds. *Hattiesburg Dailey Progress*, December 5, 1902, Vol. IV, No. 7

O. M. Maddox of Sandersville and Miss Madaline Martin of this city were married at the Baptist Church yesterday evening at 3 o'clock, Rev. I. P. Trotter officiating. The young people have the harty congratulations of their many friends in this city and Sandersville.
Hattiesburg Dailey Progress, December 16, 1902, Vol. IV, No. 16

Miss Addie McElroy, daughter of R. M. McElroy who holds a prominent position with the Gulf and Ship Island depot at this place, was married Sunday evening at 3 o'clock to W. E. Cook, a prominent young man employed at the Newman mill. They were married at the home of Brother Backus, that gentleman performing the ceremony. The young couple, who start out in life under the favorable auspices, have the hearty congratulations of their friends in the city, none wishing them greater happiness than the Progress.
Hattiesburg Dailey Progress, December 16, 1902, Vol. IV, No. 16

There was a quiet marriage at the home of the bride's father, Mr. Poole, near this city yesterday, the contracting parties being J. T. Gandy and Miss Virgie Poole, Rev. E. J. Currie officiating. The young people have the hearty congratulations of their many friends.
Hattiesburg Dailey Progress, December 22, 1902, Vol. IV, No. 21

Larkin Bounds and miss Hattie Fuller and George McCrory and miss Missouri Steel, both couples living in the country, came to town yesterday, secured license and were married on the spot, returning home rejoicing.
Hattiesburg Dailey Progress, December 23, 1902, Vol. IV, No. 22

On the afternoon of December 22, Dr. W. H. Frizzell, Jr., was united in marriage at the Main Street Methodist Church to Miss Bessie Crosby. The occasion was one of considerable interest in this city where the fair and lovely bride is deservedly popular. Dr. Frizzell is a prominent young physician of Brookhaven and is in all respects one of nature's noblemen. The fair bride is one of Hattiesburg's most charming young ladies and is the stepdaughter of Rev. W. H. Huntley. The young people have the best wishes of the Progress.
Hattiesburg Dailey Progress, December 29, 1902, Vol. IV, No. 27

Tomorrow night at 8 o'clock at the Episcopal Church, E. D. Smith of this city will lead to the marriage altar Miss Jennie Ferguson, sister of S. J. Ferguson, Passenger Conductor on the Northeastern Railroad, a beautiful young lady who has been visiting her sister, Mrs. J. W. Bolton, for a number of months. The many friends of the young couple will doubtless extend hearty congratulations in advance and wish them, as the Progress heartily does, a long and happy life. *Hattiesburg Dailey Progress*, January 6, 1903, Vol. IV, No. 34

Friends and relatives were surprised last night when it was learned that Miss Bertha Myer and J. J. Waits had married. While it was thought that such would occur, its sudden approach was not anticipated. No one witnessed the ceremony except a few friends, not even the bride's closest relatives were aware of the surprise. Miss Myer is the daughter of Mr. J. A. Myer, one of Hattiesburg's most highly respected citizens. Mr. Waits is a young man destined someday to be one of Mississippi's most influential men. He is a partner of the Fain Grocery Company and manager of the Sumrall Mercantile Company. To the bride we extend our best wishes, to the groom our heartiest congratulations. The ceremony was performed at the Methodist parsonage at 8 o'clock last night, Rev. W. M. Sullivan officiating. The happy couple left this morning for Sumrall, their future home. *Hattiesburg Dailey Progress,* January 22, 1903, Vol. IV, No. 48

Quite a surprise was sprung on friends last night by Burk Jones and Miss Charlie Wagoner. The young couple left their homes supposedly for church and returned by the home of Rev. Currie, where they were united in matrimony. Mr. Jones is a popular young man, well known in the city and superintendent of the waterworks. To him friends extend their most hearty congratulations. Miss Wagoner is too well known to need an introduction or even words of commendation in Hattiesburg. To her the best of all and the happiest life is wished. Mr. and Mrs. Jones will make their future home in this city. The best wishes of friends are extended to the happy couple.
Hattiesburg Dailey Progress, January 31, 1903, Vol. IV, No. 56

Mrs. M. E. Walley, wife of J. H. Walley, passed away yesterday evening after a lingering illness of a year's standing, caused by internal cancer. Mrs. Walley had a host of friends in Hattiesburg who, with her husband and relatives, will mourn her sad though not unexpected death. The funeral will take place this evening from the family residence, Rev. I. P. Trotter, officiating. The internment will be made at the city graveyard. The Progress joins numerous friends in extending condolence to the bereaved husband in the sad hour of his deep grief.
Hattiesburg Dailey Progress, January 31, 1903, Vol. IV, No. 56

A. W. Carter and Mrs. Mollie Coleman were quietly married in this vicinity last Friday. May their pathway through life be flowery.
Hattiesburg Dailey Progress, February 7, 1903, Vol. IV, No. 62

The Progress regrets to chronicle the death of W. B. Burkett yesterday, who has been in feeble health for some time. *Hattiesburg Dailey Progress*, February 20, 1903, Vol. IV, No. 73

A sad death came to the home of Mrs. J. W. Nance last Saturday. Little James Sidney Nance, her beloved nine-year-old son, died after struggling between life and death for several days. The funeral took place from the family residence yesterday at 3 o'clock, Rev. I. P. Trotter conducting the services, when the remains were gently laid to rest in the city cemetery. This was sad for the fact that the little fellow was such a bright boy, so kind and gentle and so dearly loved by the entire family. *Hattiesburg Dailey Progress*, March 16, 1903, Vol. IV, No. 93

J. C. Magruder, it is stated, has a fine boy at his home, arriving a night or two ago. Of course Mr. Magruder is stepping high. *Hattiesburg Dailey Progress*, March 28, 1903, Vol. IV, No. 99

Rev. E. J. Curry was called to Augusta yesterday to conduct the funeral service of Webb McDonald. Mr. McDonald was a young man and of good standing, being clerk of the Baptist church at that place. *Hattiesburg Dailey Progress*, April 21, 1903, Vol. IV, No. 124

Mrs. Riley Davis, aged 63 years, died of paralysis yesterday at 1:30 p.m. at the home of her daughter, Mrs. Charles Extine, about 3 miles south of the city. She leaves a husband and several children and grandchildren to mourn their loss. The remains were interred in the Gillis cemetery this afternoon at 2 o'clock. The Progress extends sympathies to the bereaved.
Hattiesburg Dailey Progress, April 30, 1903, Vol. IV, No. 132

Births, Deaths, and Marriages

1911 - 1920

Born to Mr. and Mrs. G. W. Dossett, Saturday, the 20th, a daughter.
The Perry County News, April 25, 1912, Vol. I, No. 12

Miss Florence McSwain of New Augusta and Mr. Michael Urban of McElroy, Louisiana, were married in the Methodist Church on Tuesday, the 28th, at 3 p.m. Rev. Robert Fykes, pastor of the church at Richton, officiating. The building was beautifully garlanded with strands of spring flowers, chosen and artistically hung for the occasion. The marriage party was aided by three maids of honor attended by their best men. Emma Ray Risher playing the part of Cupid while the beautiful strains of Mendelssohn's Wedding March rendered by Miss Alberta McSwain. The bride was elegantly gowned in white massaline, with orange blossoms, and veil and the maids wore lavender massaline, with mop caps. After the ceremony, the bride and groom took the 4:45 train for Mobile, from which city they will go to their future home at McElroy. These young people carry with them the esteem and best wishes of the entire population of New Augusta; and this paper hopes the shadows may never grow dark or dim in the highway of their life's journey.
The Perry County News, May 30, 1912, Vol. I, No. 16

A telephone message last Sunday morning brought to relatives and friends the sad intelligence of the death of Mrs. L. M. *{Emma Rae}* Risher, which occurred at her home in Natchez Sunday morning at 7 o'clock. She was a daughter of Mrs. Bella McSwain of this place and has many relatives here. She had been in Natchez only a month, having spent the spring and summer with relatives here, and the news of her death came as a shock to everyone. Besides other relatives, she leaves a sorrowing husband, two children, mother, three sisters and four brothers. Her body was brought back here and laid to rest in the family burial ground Monday afternoon at 5 o'clock. The funeral services were held at the church and were conducted in a beautiful and impressive manner by Rev. E. J. Currie of Hattiesburg.
The Perry County News, August 15, 1912, Vol. I, No. 27

Eugene Story and Miss Daisy Jones were married at the home of the bride's parents, Mr. and Mrs. R. H. Jones, at Mahned, last Thursday night. Rev. Stapp performed the marriage ceremony. The wedding was a quiet home affair, only a few intimate friends being present. The young couple have both for quite a while made their home at Mahned, Miss Jones having been Post-mistress and Mr. Story is an employee of Kennedy Bros. at that place. They left for Durant and other points to visit relatives. *The Perry County News,* October 5, 1912, Vol. I, No. 34

Mr. C. C. Dearman and Miss Bella Burkett were married Wednesday night at the home of the bride's mother at Amory, Miss. Mr. Dearman is the popular and efficient sheriff of Perry County and is too well known to need any word the News might say as to his integrity and popularity as a man or an officer. Miss Burkett was for quite a long time a valued employee of the Anderson Mercantile Company at Richton, and is a young woman possessing all the qualities which go to make up a cultured, refined, true and loving wife. The couple returned this morning and will make this their home. The News joins their many friends in wishing them a prosperous married life. *The Perry County News,* November 9, 1912, Vol. I, No. 42

H. C. McSwain died at his home between Wingate and Hintonville last Wednesday afternoon at 2 o'clock. He had been sick for about seven weeks. One daughter and three sons survive him. His body was interred in the family cemetery near the home. A number of relatives and friends from this place attended the burial Thursday morning.
The Perry County News, January 4, 1913, Vol. I, No. 50

A pretty home wedding of this week was that of J. N. McCoy and Miss Minnie Nichols, which took place at the home of the bride's parents at Mahned, Wednesday afternoon. Rev. A. L. O'Bryant of Hattiesburg performed the ceremony. A number of friends and relatives were present. Mr. McCoy is our popular deputy sheriff and is a young man of admirable character. His bride is one of the most popular young ladies of her neighborhood and has a host of friends at this place. The News joins their many friends in wishing them many years of wedded bliss.
The Perry County News, January 25, 1913, Vol. II, No. 1

Edward Lucien Cowan was born in Pass Christian, Harrison County, Miss., Sept. 22, 1883. He was the eldest son of R. G. and Bella Gertrude Adams Cowan. On Apr. 5, 1906 he was happily married to Miss Susie Belle Fullilove. They shared the joys and sorrows of life together till Feb. 10, 1913, when, after many weary months he had suffered from a dreaded malady which had baffled the physicians skill, and which perhaps none alone could surely and permanently eradicate, the man of childlike faith stood the storm of life's rugged path and laid himself down without a murmur, to await with submissive patience, sublime attitude and an inspiring Christian resignation, the final call. Brother Cowan was a Pharmacist by profession, having followed that line of work from his boyhood. He was a member of the Methodist Episcopal Church, South. A man of pleasant demeanor and easy to approach. His virtues commanded respect and admiration of all who knew him. If your acquaintance with him did not extend to the fireside it was your misfortune and no fault of his hospitality. He was a true friend and a modest Christian gentleman. He was a devoted son, a gentle husband, and affectionate father, and a loyal brother. If we were to measure his days by lovable and noble qualities of heart and mind, and by obedience to their suggestions, then his life was long and full, though; the sun has gone down in the morning, as we reckon our periods. I shall cherish pleasant recollections of him and am glad to think that when the remorseless enemy approached death had no terror and his faith was strong. The enemy conquered his body but the soul went (*the rest of this line is unreadable*). After services in the Methodist Church conducted by his Pastor, his body was laid to rest with Masonic honors in the McSwain cemetery. He leaves a father, three brothers, four sisters, a wife and child and a host of friends and loved ones to morn his death. May the Lord comfort the bereaved with the blessed assurance that while they cannot bring him back they can go to him and dwell with him forever through Jesus Christ our Lord. His Pastor, C. J. Stapp
The Perry County News, February 13, 1913, Vol. II, No. 4

A wedding of unusual interest to her friends here was that of Miss Minnie Lee Mathis of Beaumont to Mr. Luther H. Cole. The marriage occurred at the home of the bride's father, Dr. E. J. Mathis Wednesday morning at 8 o'clock, Rev. C. J. Stapp officiating. The couple left immediately for Tampa, Fla., where they will reside.
The Perry County News, March 13, 1913, Vol. II, No. 8

A wedding of much interest to their many friends was that last Sunday afternoon of Hon. D. K. McDonald and Mrs. Ethel Dearman. The marriage occurred at the home of the bride at 4 o'clock. Rev. J. N. McMillin performed the ceremony in the presence of the immediate relatives and a few friends. *The Perry County News,* March 27, 1913, Vol. II, No. 10

The infant daughter of Joe Howard and wife died Thursday morning. It was buried in the Sweetwater cemetery, Friday morning. *The Perry County News,* April 10, 1913, Vol. II, No. 12

A wedding of interest occurred last Sunday morning when Henry Morren and Miss Lizzie Mixon were united in matrimony. The ceremony was performed in Hattiesburg. The couple having gone up there on the 10:32 train. As it was a Gretna Green affair, only a few of the most intimate friends were aware of the approaching event. The News extends to them heartiest congratulations. *The Perry County News,* June 5, 1913, Vol. II, No. 21

Mr. W. A. McKenzie died at his home a few miles above Mahned last Tuesday and was buried at the family burial ground Wednesday morning. He was one of the best and most substantial citizens of the county. *The Perry County News,* June 19, 1913, Vol. II, No. 22

Judge H. S. Brown performed his first marriage ceremony last Thursday when he tied the knot for J. S. Stutts and Mary E. Wilkins. He seemed to make a good job of it as the happy couple went on their way rejoicing. *The Perry County News,* June 19, 1913, Vol. II, No. 22

Alex McKenzie was born in Perry County, Mississippi, March 22, 1850, and died at his home near Mahned June 17, 1913. His life was spent in his native county. He was from one of the best families and one of the first in his community. He did his own thinking and had the courage of his convictions. He was found on the right side of moral issues. He joined the church sometime in early manhood and at the time of his death was an efficient steward in the M. E. C. S. In middle life he was married to Miss Alice Cook of Jasper County. They lived happily together until his death. He left a wife, two daughters, one son, three brothers, three sisters, and a host of friends to mourn his loss. But they are not without hope. He died as he had lived with a strong and abiding faith in Christ. He was a good citizen, a true friend and brother, kind and devoted to his wife and children, and loyal and generous to his church. We shall miss him here, but by God's grace we expect to see him again. C. J. Stapp
The Perry County News, June 26, 1913, Vol. II, No. 23

Miss Nannie Nutt Batchelor died at the hospital in the City of Vicksburg on Thursday, July 17, 1913. She was buried in the Phillips-Batchelor Lot in the cemetery at Vicksburg. Miss Batchelor was born at Rodney, in this state, but had made her home in New Augusta for a number of years. *The Perry County News,* August 7, 1913, Vol. II, No. 29

Amos Jordan, of Kittrell, is the happy father of two fine baby boys. One weighing eight pounds and the other nine pounds. *The Perry County News,* January 22, 1914, Vol. III, No. 1

A marriage of more than usual interest to the people of this part of the county was that of Mr. H. A. Forgey to Miss Mary Overstreet, which took place at the home of the bride's brother, J. H. Overstreet, at Beaumont on Wednesday afternoon of last week. They will remain in Beaumont, where their many friends join in wishing them a happy wedded life.
The Perry County News, July 30, 1914, Vol. III, No. 29

Miss Blanche Dominick left Sunday for New Orleans where she was joined in marriage Tuesday morning at 10:30 o'clock to Paul D. Bereau of Lafayette, La. The marriage took place in the private parlor at the Grunewald Hotel. The bride has been one of the most popular young ladies of this place during her residence here, being the daughter of the recent Pastor, Rev. W. D. Dominick. The groom is a prominent young business man of Lafayette, La. and is highly regarded at his hometown. The News joins the many friends of Miss Blanche in wishing them a happy and prosperous married life. *The Perry County News,* August 27, 1914, Vol. III, No. 33

A new boy came to bless the home of Mr. and Mrs. Albert Burnett last Sunday morning.
The Richton Dispatch, August 28, 1914, Vol. IX, No. 4

Will Jones and wife are proud of their new arrival, little Miss Jones, who took up her abode with them Wednesday. *The Richton Dispatch,* September 4, 1914, Vol. IX, No. 5

Sunday afternoon the Death Angel visited the home of A. J. Meadows, claiming their six year old son. A large host of friends and relatives extend their sympathy in this their hour of deepest trouble. *The Richton Dispatch,* September 4, 1914, Vol. IX, No. 5

Hubert Davis and Miss Lillie Brewer were married last Sunday evening at the home of the Bride's parents, leaving Monday for Lucedale, their future home.
The Richton Dispatch, September 11, 1914, Vol. IX, No. 6

One of the prettiest weddings noticed recently was that of Mr. Jimmie Breland and Miss Leila Goff, which took place at the bride's home near Leaf, on Sunday, September 27. The bridal party, consisting of Miss Ollie Breland and Mr. John Pipkins, Miss Bettie Reeves and Mr. Ervin Goff, and the bride and groom, marched up to the table spread under the trees in the yard where Dr. Bliss Green awaited them. After an impressive ceremony, the party sat down to an elaborate wedding dinner. About four o'clock the party left for Mr. Calvin Breland's home, where a handsome infair supper was spread. After the large crowd had joined in good wishes, the wedding cakes were cut, and the people returned home to dream over the cake and await the next couple. *The Perry County News,* October 1, 1914, Vol. III, No. 38

Miss Eran, the sixteen year old daughter of T. P. Palmer of Hintonville, died last Thursday night after a lingering illness of several months.
The Richton Dispatch, October 9, 1914, Vol. IX, No. 9

Quite an unusual wedding was celebrated here on Sunday, when Mr. Rasmus R. Goff and Miss Thelma Breland were joined in matrimony. The groom and his attendants ran up on horseback to Mr. Calvin Breland's residence. Upon their dismounting, they were ushered into the parlor where the bride and her attendants awaited them.

After a short wait, the party, consisting of Mr. Icham Breland and Miss Mary Pittman, Mr. John Pipkins and Miss Ollie Breland, and the bride and groom, were all conducted to the head of the wedding table by a string band consisting of Messrs, Julius Herring and Gary and Bob Davis. Then Supervisor P. E. Cochran tied the nuptial knot. The party then sat down to a most enjoyable dinner. The many friends of this couple join in wishing them a long and happy life together.
The Perry County News, November 26, 1914, Vol. III, No. 46

O. C. Clark of Estabutcha and Miss Ella Smith of Richton were quietly married at Hattiesburg last Sunday night and are now making their home at the home of Mr. Clark. We wish for them a long and prosperous journey through life.
The Richton Dispatch, October 16, 1914, Vol. IX, No. 11

Columbus Breland, who it was stated in last week's issue of the News, was critically ill at the Infirmary in Hattiesburg, died at that place last Sunday night. His body was carried back home, and on Tuesday was laid to rest in the family burial ground a few miles south of his home which is near Barbara. A large crowd attended the funeral services which were conducted by Rev. Mr. Glynn. Mr. Breland was a well and favorably known man of his section, and had many friends here, quite a number of whom attended the burial.
The Perry County News, December 3, 1914, Vol. III, No. 47

Born to J. F. Beasley and wife on Monday, March 29, a 12 pound boy.
The Perry County News, April 1, 1915, Vol. IV, No. 18

A beautiful Easter gift in the form of a baby boy came to gladden the home of Mr. And Mrs. J. N. McCoy last Sunday. He will be called James Nichols.
The Perry County News, April 8, 1915, Vol. IV, No. 19

The many friends of Dr. and Mrs. W. A. Young formerly of this place but now of Louisville will be interested to know of the birth of a little daughter who came to them a few days ago.
The Perry County News, April 8, 1915, Vol. IV, No. 19

The friends of Myrt Wright, who made his home here for some time, but who has been at Louisville for the past year, will be grieved to learn of his death, which occurred on Saturday, March 27, from Typhoid Fever. His aged father died the day following from the same malady.
The Perry County News, April 8, 1915, Vol. IV, No. 19

Mr. Adolph Gillis and Miss Kate McKenzie were married at the home of the bride's father Wednesday. *The Perry County News,* April 22, 1915, Vol. IV, No. 21

Born to Mr. And Mrs. S. M. Shattles, on last Wednesday, a fine baby boy.
The Perry County News, April 22, 1915, Vol. IV, No. 21

Mrs. Sarah Elizabeth Kennedy, who had been so ill since she was burned four months ago, passed away last Sunday morning at 5 o'clock and was buried in Denham cemetery Monday morning. Mrs. Kennedy had reached the 83rd milestone on life's journey, and each year had been filled with kind words, kind thoughts, and loving deeds.

She was loved by all who knew her for the humble simplicity and gentleness of her nature. In her life's record, there is not one charge of her having ever spoken evil of anyone. Having been left a widow during the civil war, she had a hard struggle to rear five little children, all of whom are now living and are a credit to their mother's training. She also reared a younger sister, Miss Margaret Denham, who was left an orphan at an early age. Mrs. Kennedy will be sadly missed not only in the home, but by every friend and neighbor and even by the young girls of the town who often visited her. Being too feeble to get out any, she was ever ready to give to old and young alike a kindly welcome and gentle word when they visited her. The funeral services were conducted by her pastor, Rev. J. W. Allen and a large concourse of relatives and friends viewed the loved form and saw it tenderly lowered to its last resting place. The News extends its deepest sympathies to the grief stricken relatives.
The Perry County News, August 12, 1915, Vol. IV, No. 37

As the News goes to press, a message from Jackson hospital announces the death of John Havens who was operated on there for appendicitis. The body will arrive here for burial today.
The Perry County News, October 28, 1915, Vol. IV, No. 48

A little daughter was born to Mr. and Mrs. A. J. Ikerd on last Monday.
The Perry County News, November 18, 1915, Vol. IV, No. 51

Friends of L. M. Risher will be interested in learning of his marriage, Wednesday to Miss Maggie Guringer of Alexandria. La. *The Perry County News,* December 9, 1915, Vol. V, No. 2

W. R. Whatley and Miss Abbie Breland were married last Sunday at the home of the bride at Kittrell. A big supper was served after the ceremony to which a large number of friends and relatives were invited. *The Perry County News,* December 30, 1915, Vol. V, No. 5

Mrs. Lou Pearce died at her home near Red Hill church last Sunday, after an illness of only a few days. She was buried in the family cemetery, Monday morning, a large crowd of friends and relatives being present. Her Pastor, Rev. C. M. Grayson, conducted the funeral services.
The Perry County News, January 6, 1916, Vol. V, No. 6

A little son was born to R. E. and Mrs. Lelia Selby, last Saturday, January 8th.
The Perry County News, January 13, 1916, Vol. V, No. 7

God called sister Lou Pearce last first Sunday, January 2, to that upper and better kingdom. She was born in 1859 and died at her home in Perry County. She was 56 years, 11 months, and 26 days old. She was a good and kind mother in her home and she was loved by her children and by her neighbors. All who knew her personally soon learned to love her. She loved her church and she always gave her prayers and presence to the services at Red Hill Church where she was a member at the time of her death. While it is the writer's privilege to preach to 1100 members in the six churches that he now supplies, out of all this number, sister Pearce will be greatly and constantly missed by him in his work. She was laid to rest Monday, January 3, in the family cemetery, the writing officiating. She leaves six children, six brothers and sisters and a host of relatives and friends to mourn her death. May God be glorified in the sad hearts of those who weep for her.

But let us not weep as those who have no hope. May God bless all of her loved ones is the prayer of her Pastor. C. M. Grayson *The Perry County News,* January 13, 1916, Vol. V, No. 7

J. A. Stafford and Mrs. Lula Vance were married at 10 o'clock at the home of the bride's father, F. Howard. Both parties are well known here. Mr. Stafford being one of the county's prosperous farmers, while the bride is a daughter of Mr. F. Howard, also one of staunchest rural citizens. The News wishes them every happiness.
The Perry County News, January 20, 1916, Vol. V, No. 8

Mrs. Lula Gill died Monday night at her home a few miles southeast of town. The body was carried to Hattiesburg on the morning train Tuesday and interred in the old home cemetery a few miles from that place. The deceased leaves four children, Mack and Rufus Gill and Mrs. Irene Blankenship, all of near this place and a married daughter from near Hattiesburg, whose name the News failed to get. *The Perry County News,* January 27, 1916, Vol. V, No. 9

The News deeply sympathies with Scott Myers, who is with the J. F. Ruffin Co., in the death of his sister, Miss Della, who died very suddenly at their home near Hattiesburg Tuesday night. Scott was notified by telephone and went up Wednesday morning to attend the funeral.
The Perry County News, February 3, 1916, Vol. V, No. 10

Mr. and Mrs. F. F. Myers announce the engagement and approaching marriage of their daughter Lois to Mr. William R. Zimmerman, of Benmore, Ms., on Wednesday, June 14, 1916.
The Perry County News, May 5, 1916, Vol. V, No. 23

Mr. McAllister who lived about three miles west of Indian Springs died last Friday morning and was buried in the Indian Springs cemetery on Saturday morning. He leaves his wife and one child besides many friends who sadly miss him.
The Perry County News, May 19, 1916, Vol. V, No. 25

J. P. Sapp, one of the pioneer citizens of the county, died at his home at Runnelstown, Tuesday after an illness of more than two months. He was buried at that place Wednesday. He leaves a large family. *The Perry County News,* May 26, 1916, Vol. V, No. 26

Mr. Evan Garraway died at his mother's home in Richton last Monday following a long illness from Tuberculosis. He was very prominently connected throughout the county, being a son of the late Hon. S. T. Garraway and Mrs. Emma Stevens Garraway. His body was brought to Old Augusta for interment Tuesday afternoon. He leaves a mother, two small children, a sister and two brothers besides numerous other relatives. His wife died several years ago.
The Perry County News, May 26, 1916, Vol. V, No. 26

Mr. Andrew Carter, an aged citizen of McLaurin, died suddenly at his home last Saturday. His sister, Mrs. C. T. Fullilove, and a number of other relatives and friends from here attended the burial which took place near his home. *The Perry County News,* June 2, 1916, Vol. V, No. 27

One of the most prettiest and most interesting events which New Augusta has witnessed for many days was that which took place Wednesday afternoon at three o'clock at the home of Mr. and Mrs. F. F. Myers, when their daughter Lois, was united in marriage to William R. Zimmerman, of Benmore. The lawn had been artistically decorated for the occasion, pink and green being the color motif, and it was there, under an arbor of soft, clinging vines, relieved by dainty bows and streamers of pink, to the soft strains of Mendelssohn's Wedding March, that the couple took upon themselves the world old, yet ever new vows, to Love, Honor, and Cherish. Just before the ceremony, Miss Cora Cook sang "Until," while little John Stevens McLaurin and Dorothy Dossett, nephew and niece of the bride, formed an aisle out of pink streamers for the bridal party. Then during Lohengrin's Bridal Chorus, rendered by Mrs. T. L. McWilliams, Misses Bessie and Cora Cook, the bridal party approached the arbor. First came Miss Leo, sister and only bridesmaid of the bride, wearing a dress of white net with pink trimmings and a chiffon picture hat of white and pink, and carrying a large cluster of pink Klarney roses. She was followed by little Emily Dossett, four year old niece of the bride, a veritable fairy in white and pink, bearing a basket of white and pink rose petals which she strewed in the pathway. The bride came last: beautiful in a gown of white chiffon with ruffles of taffeta, her head adorned with a lovely hat of Georgiette crepe, with whit plumes, and bearing an armful of Bride's roses, Lillies-of-the-valley, and orange blossoms. They were met at the bridal alter by Frank Zimmerman, best man and brother of the groom, William R. Zimmerman, who joined his bride there, and Rev. J. N. McMillin, officiating minister, all of whom had entered by a side entrance. After a few well-chosen words by the minister, the ring was presented to the groom, who drew it on the finger of his bride, and they were pronounced man and wife. Immediately after the ceremony, refreshments were served and a tiny bride knot of pink and green pinned on each guest. The young couple left about four o'clock for New Orleans and other points where they will visit relatives for a few days before going to their home at Benmore. The News wishes that their married life may have just enough shadow to temper the glare of the sun.
The Perry County News, June 16, 1916, Vol. V, No. 29

Cupid has again been on the job. Last Saturday afternoon, Will Sellers of Beaumont and Miss Lydia Dennis of this place went to the Hotel at Wingate and were quietly married. They then went on to their home at Beaumont. The marriage was such a surprise to most of their friends that they at first took it as a joke, only two or three of the most fortunate ones having any knowledge of the approaching event. *The Perry County News,* June 30, 1916, Vol. V, No. 31

G. W. Louis and Miss Alma Cowan stole a march on their friends here and met in Hattiesburg and got married a few days ago. They are making their home for the present at the White house. The News wishes for them that they may continue as happy all the way thru life as they appear now to be. *The Perry County News,* July 7, 1916, Vol. V, No. 32

News was received here a few days ago of the death of J. O. McDonald, of Prescott, Ark. He formerly lived at Bellville and was well known here. He had been in ill health for several months with Bright's disease. *The Perry County News,* May 24, 1918, Vol. VII, No. 26

The entire community sympathizes with Mr. Albert Davis in his deep sorrow. Just three months ago his little eight year old daughter died after only a few hours illness with spinal meningitis. Ten days later his wife passed away with the same dread disease. Last Sunday his eighteen months old baby boy, Jeff Rogers, died of colitis. It seems that his sorrow is more than should fall to the lot of one, for only a few months ago he suffered heavy financial losses thru the destruction of a saw mill in which he was interested.
The Perry County News, May 24, 1918, Vol. VII, No. 26

Slowly but surely the devastation of war creeps upon us and takes its toll in the death of our loved ones. Five of Perry County's boys have given their lives thru disease in the cantonments, thereby making the supreme sacrifice for their country. The last of these was Albert L. Myers, son of Mrs. Belle Myers of this place. He was born July 16, 1895, being a little less than 23 years of age. A young man just entering the realm of usefulness of perfect physique and possessing the unbounded admiration of all who knew him, it is difficult to understand why we should be deprived of his life and active influence just now, but his call came, and after an illness from pneumonia with which he struggled for one week, he gave up the battle and entered that life of eternal PEACE. The end came at 3:50 on the morning of May 16, in the camp hospital at Newport News, Va. Several years ago he made a public profession of Christianity and united with the Presbyterian Church of which he remained a consistent member until his death. Last summer he answered his country's call and enlisted with the 653 Aero Squadron. He left home on August 21st last, and was in New Orleans for several months, after which his company was sent to Virginia where it still remains. Guy Garraway, a cousin, and a member of the same company, brought the body home and the funeral service was held in the Presbyterian Church last Sunday afternoon at 3:30 o'clock. Pastors Allen and Ramsey of the Presbyterian and Methodist churches, respectively, conducted the service, after which he was laid to rest with military honors in the Denham cemetery at Mahned. The church was filled to its utmost capacity, the back of it being reserved for the colored friends, who attested their friendship for Albert in their humble way. Numerous and beautiful were the floral offerings, the casket and altar being literally covered in them. Especially pretty and touching was the immense wreath presented by his company, into which was delicately woven the national colors. Two American flags were crossed upon the casket and one softly draped across his chest.
The Perry County News, May 24, 1918, Vol. VII, No. 26

Mrs. Jane Hinton, widow of the late William Hinton, died at the family residence near Wingate Tuesday afternoon, after an illness of several days duration. "Aunt Jane" was one of the oldest inhabitants in the county and was well known and well loved by all, and especially by the older acquaintances and settlers. She leaves a family of four children, all grown and married. They are: J. J., of Wingate; Henry, in military service; Mesdames Belle Matthews, of Wingate; and Mattie McCoy, of Richton. One son and two daughters have died within the last few years. "Uncle Billy" and "Aunt Jane" Hinton were people of fine character and were useful citizens and as people, such as these, quietly slip away, one by one, the community sustains in each an irreparable loss. The News tenders its sympathy to those bereaved.
The Perry County News, June 7, 1918, Vol. VII, No. 28

Another one of Perry County's quota in the service of Uncle Sam has made the supreme sacrifice. A message came Monday morning to H. H. Mixon conveying the sad intelligence of the sudden death of his son, Lee S. Mixon. From what we can learn, his death followed a sudden and severe attack of pneumonia. He was in the last draft call and left here only three or four weeks ago for the A. & M. College to take training by the Government for some specific work. His body was brought home and laid to rest in the family cemetery about 8 miles north of town Tuesday afternoon. Rev. J. W. Ramsey conducted a short service at the grave after which he was buried with military honors. The grief stricken parents, brothers, sisters, and other relatives and friends have the deepest sympathy of the News.
The Perry County News, June 14, 1918, Vol. VII, No. 29

Mrs. W. B. Harry, who had for several days been critically ill at the home of her son S. F. Harry here, died at 5 o'clock this Friday morning. The body has been embalmed and will be taken to the old family home at Garlandsville for burial.
The Perry County News, July 5, 1918, Vol. VII, No. 32

Born to Rev. and Mrs. W. L. McCardle – a girl.
The Perry County News, July 12, 1918, Vol. VII, No. 33

Mr. and Mrs. C. C. Johnson, of Sanford, have announced to their Friends here the birth on July 11 of a son. Mrs. Johnson will be remembered as Miss Iris McNiell, formerly of this place.
The Perry County News, July 19, 1918, Vol. VII, No. 34

Mr. and Mrs. J. E. Pearce of the Red Hill Community were the recipients of a baby son several days ago. *The Perry County News,* August 9, 1918, Vol. VII, No. 37

Ira B. Cochran and wife are happy over the arrival of a little son in their home. Mrs. Cochran will be remembered as Miss Terrie Ferguson.
The Perry County News, August 9, 1918, Vol. VII, No. 37

A marriage of interest was that of Hugh Atchinson and Miss Inez Hinton, which occurred at the home of the bride's father, at Wingate, Wednesday night. Justice R. Kittrell officiated.
The Perry County News, September 13, 1918, Vol. VII, No. 42

Friends here will be interested in learning of the marriage at Los Angeles, Cal. on August 7th, of John Hugh Davis, Jr. and Miss Blanche Lyttle, of Miami, Arizona. Hugh is the youngest son of Judge and Mrs. J. H. Davis of this place and has scores of personal friends, for to know him is to be his friend. He is now in the service of his Uncle, being a member of 4th Training Battery F. A. C. O. T. S., Camp Taylor, Louisville, Ky. Miss Lyttle is an attractive and accomplished young woman and while not known personally here, she is reputed to be in every way a fitting companion for the man of her choice. The News joins the many friends in extending congratulations. *The Perry County News,* September 13, 1918, Vol. VII, No. 42

Mr. D. D. Hairston and Miss Edna Jones were quietly married last Sunday morning at the home of the bride's parents at Mahned. Rev. J. W. Ramsey performed the ceremony after which the happy couple left for a brief trip to Vaiden, the old home of the groom. Mr. Hairston is a member of one of the most prosperous business firms in this section of the country and has lived here too long and is too well known to need any eulogy from the News. The bride has made her home at this place and at Mahned for several years and has scores of friends. She spent one year as saleslady for Hairston Bros. And it was during that time that Cupid put in his master strokes. For several months past she has been the efficient depot agent at Mahned. They returned home Wednesday and are domiciled in the residence recently vacated by H. C. Hughes and family. The News extends congratulations and wishes for them a life of happiness and prosperity.
The Perry County News, November 1, 1918, Vol. VII, No. 49

Mr. W. B. Harry passed away last Sunday morning at eleven o'clock, after an illness of seven weeks. His condition seemed considerably improved some ten days ago and his friends and loved ones hoped for a complete recovery; but on account of his weakened condition and his age his effort and struggle for lost strength failed. Sunday morning as easily and gently as a child might fall asleep in its mother's arms, he breathed his last, and his spirit wafted its way back to the God who gave it. "Father" Harry, as he was affectionately called by his friends, came here, with his wife, about one year ago to make his home with his only son, S. F. Harry; and by the kindly, sympathetic and truly cultured manner of the couple, which was emblematic of the meek and lowly Nazarene; they won the friendship and esteem of all with whom they came in contact. His wife preceded him to the better world a little more than three months ago. Mr. Harry was 65 years of age and had been a Christian and a loyal member of the Presbyterian Church for many years. His body was carried to the old home, Garlandsville, for interment, accompanied by S. F. Harry and family and Mrs. E. J. Griffin.
The Perry County News, November 1, 1918, Vol. VII, No. 49

Friends here will be interested to learn of the recent arrival of a little daughter to Mr. and Mrs. Holt Myers of Dothan. Ala. *The Perry County News,* November 22, 1918, Vol. VII, No. 52

Mr. F. F. Hinton died at his home at Wingate at 3:30 o'clock Thursday morning, after several weeks illness with influenza. A few days ago his condition seemed so much improved that he was thought to be out of danger; but last Sunday he developed pneumonia and in his already weakened condition he soon succumbed to the malady. His body was laid to rest this (Friday) morning in the Nichols cemetery, near Mr. Hinton's old home a few miles above old Augusta. His pastor, Reverend J. N. McMillin conducted the funeral service which was attended by many relatives and friends. *The Perry County News,* November 22, 1918, Vol. VII, No. 52

A telegram came last Tuesday afternoon announcing the death of Tom Pearce, a well- known and popular young man of the Red Hill Community, which occurred in France October 17, from that fatal malady pneumonia. He had been a soldier in the regular army for a number of years when our country entered the war and like thousands of other brave fellows, did not hesitate to take his chances with the rest. *The Perry County News,* November 29, 1918, Vol. VIII, No. 1

Mrs. E. I. McSwain, of Hattiesburg, who is well known and widely connected here and at surrounding places, received the news a few days ago that her only son, Robert, had died in France. He had been across only a short time and the last communication from him stated that he was in perfect health. The News extends sympathy to the mother and sisters and the many other relatives. *The Perry County News,* November 29, 1918, Vol. VIII, No. 1

Mr. Thomas E. Hinton, an aged citizen of the county and who lived out a few miles from Beaumont, died at an infirmary in Mobile last Thursday night. His body was brought home by his son M. M. Hinton, and laid at rest Friday afternoon in the family burying ground. Reverend M. W. Franklin, of Washington, Greene County, conducted the funeral service. Mr. Hinton was one of the best citizens of Perry County, and as the case of "Uncle Jack" Thomas, David B. Whatley and many other of the older and more substantial citizens who have recently passed away, his place will be hard to fill. He leaves several children, among whom are, M. M. Hinton of Agness, Mrs. W. W. Greene of McLain, Mrs. H. C. McDonald of Beaumont, and Mrs. J. P. Garraway of Mahned. *The Perry County News,* November 29, 1918, Vol. VIII, No. 1

On last Saturday afternoon R. Ferguson received a message stating that his son Robert had died in France on October 9, from wounds received in battle. The young man joined the State Guards as a volunteer in 1916, and was mustered out in 1917, and immediately joined the National Guards. In November of that year he was sent with his Company to help settle the strike difficulties in the oil fields of Louisiana and Texas. He was sent from there to Camp Beauregard where he remained until he was drawn in the replacement draft in June of this year and sent overseas. Only one letter was received from him after he had landed over in France, and it was dated early in July. Robert was very popular with the younger set within his circle of acquaintances and will be greatly missed by them.
The Perry County News, December 13, 1918, Vol. VIII, No. 3

Born to Mr. and Mrs. C. C. Hairston on December 14, a boy.
The Perry County News, December 20, 1918, Vol. VIII, No. 4

Born to Captain and Mrs. B. T. Robinson on December 15, a girl.
The Perry County News, December 20, 1918, Vol. VIII, No. 4

Jesse O'Neal, son of J. A. O'Neal, who is one of the most prominent citizens of the south end of the county, died at his home last Saturday. He fell a victim to Spanish influenza after only a few days illness. He was an excellent young man, and his death came as a great shock to his parents and his many other relatives and friends.
The Perry County News, December 20, 1918, Vol. VIII, No. 4

Quite a shock came to the many friends of Jesse O'Neal, when on Saturday, December 14, at 3 P. M. his son was called from us. James Jesse O'Neal was born on January 31, 1900. He was the son of James A. and Melison (Breland) O'Neal. He was one of our dear home boys, well known for his cheery face and kind deeds. The interment took place in the private cemetery of the grandfather, Major O'Neal, on Sunday, December 15, Rev. Mr. Sells, of Wiggins, conducting the funeral service. May the great Father of us all send his ministering angels to comfort the bereaved family. A FRIEND. *The Perry County News,* December 20, 1918, Vol. VIII, No. 4

Our entire community was saddened when the news came that K. P. Foust had passed away at the South Mississippi Infirmary at an early hour Friday morning. Several weeks ago he had a severe attack of influenza from which he did not entirely recover. He was carried to Hattiesburg for treatment and had all done for him that science could do but in his weakened condition he contracted pneumonia and without strength to combat the disease he succumbed to it in a few hours. Possibly no man has ever come here who gained in popularity more quickly than Mr. Foust. He came here to reside about six months ago, and by his courteous, sincere and unaffected manner, his kindly smile and hearty handshake, he won his way into the hearts of old and young alike. He was a Methodist minister and until recently belonged to the Conference but gave up his work of active ministry to engage in literary teaching for he said he felt that his life's work would accomplish more if he were in position to deal more directly with young people. He occupied the pulpits here on several occasions and always his discourses were directed mainly to the boys and girls. At the beginning of his illness he was principal of the Beaumont school. He leaves a wife and two small children, his father, mother, and other relatives to mourn his loss. His wife is a daughter of Mrs. Belle Myers of this place. The News extends condolence to the bereaved ones. *The Perry County News,* January 10, 1919, Vol. VIII, No. 7

The many friends of Mr. and Mrs. W. F. Backstrom deeply sympathize with them in the loss of their thirteen months old baby girl, Lillian Gregory, who died Sunday morning at 2:30 o'clock after an illness of three days from scarlet fever. Although quite ill from the first, the little one's condition was not considered so critical until Saturday afternoon when spinal meningitis set in and she survived only a few hours. The physicians state that this particular form of meningitis is purely a sympathetic one and is not contagious. Little Lillian Gregory was an unusually bright and attractive child, and the little sparkling eyes and bewitching smile went right into one's heart. The one happy little year spent here will ever be a bright spot in the memory of the now heart-broken parents. They cannot help but feel that in choosing their baby to help adorn His kingdom, God has conferred an honor upon them for the choicest bouquets are made up largely of tiny buds, the most magnificent jewels so often contain the tiniest gems, so we would point the loving parents to Him who never makes an error and who will never leave nor forsake those who trust in Him. Interment was made in the Richton cemetery Sunday afternoon, Rev. J. N. McMillin conducting the funeral services, assisted by Rev. E. S. P'Pool, of Meridian, who is a brother of Mrs. Backstrom. *The Perry County News,* January 24, 1919, Vol. VIII, No. 9

A marriage of much interest to their many friends was that of Mr. Clinton M. Barnes and Miss Josie Nobles, both of Mahned, which happy event occurred at the home of the bride's father, last Sunday afternoon. *The Perry County News,* February 21, 1919, Vol. VIII, No. 13

Mr. and Mrs. C. R. McDonald make the informal announcement of the approaching marriage of their two eldest daughters, Miss Lela D., to Mr. William Elbert Fike, of Hattiesburg, and Miss Eva, to Mr. Archie Eugene Davis, also of Hattiesburg, the double ceremony to be solemnized by Rev. J. N. McMillin at the Baptist church at this place on Sunday, April 6, at two o'clock p.m. *The Perry County News,* March 28, 1919, Vol. VIII, No. 18

Miss Jeanette Heartsock of this place and Mr. M. L. Miller, Camp Shelby, were married in Hattiesburg last Thursday. *The Perry County News,* April 11, 1919, Vol. VIII, No. 20

Mr. Birt Grantham and Miss Etta Lewis were married at the home of the bride's parents last Sunday, Rev. R. M. Hardin officiating.
The Perry County News, April 11, 1919, Vol. VIII, No. 20

An event of unusual interest to their many friends was the marriage last Sunday afternoon of Mr. Archie Eugene Davis to Miss Eva McDonald and Mr. William Elbert Fike to Miss Lela D. McDonald, the marriage ceremony being performed at the Baptist church with Dr. J. T. Christian of Hattiesburg officiating. The church had been beautifully decorated in evergreens, with a delicate and dainty touch of the first wild flowers of early spring, honeysuckle and plum. In the pulpit was an arbor made of pink, green, and white from the top of which was suspended a large bell of the same colors, and beneath this arbor the happy couples plighted their troth, which was the blissful culmination of the romances begun several months ago. The church house was filled to its utmost capacity and the audience was in a state of joyful expectancy as Mrs. Terry and Miss McKay took their places at the organ and violin, and as Lohengrin's bridal chorus was wafted on the air the bridal procession was ushered in by Misses Lucile Williams and Ruth McLaurin. Next came the matron of honor, Mrs. H. B. McDonald, sister of the brides, gowned in a Belgian blue taffeta and carrying a bouquet of pink and white roses. Following her came the ring-bearers, little Margie and Mamie McDonald, sister and niece of the brides, daintily clad in white frocks with pink sashes and hair bows and bearing the wedding rings in little baskets of pink satin. Then came the brides, lovely in suits of midnight blue with accessories of tan each carrying an armful of bride's roses and ferns. They were met at the alter by the grooms and Dr. Christian, in a few well-spoken words in his easy yet masterful style, pronounced them husband and wife. The ceremony was made more impressive by the subdued and plaintive tones of the violin, with the organ accompaniment in 'I Love You Truly'. After the benediction had been pronounced the bridal procession passed out to the triumphant strains of Mendelsohn's Wedding march. Immediately following the ceremony the newly wedded couples left for Mobile for a few days stay before going to Hattiesburg, where they will reside. Probably no marriage has ever taken place here where the good wishes of all were more unanimously given. The brides were both born and raised here, being daughters of Mr. and Mrs. C. R. McDonald, and our town and surrounding country have never known two girls of whom they were prouder and who were more worthy of that respect and admiration than they. Both have quiet and reserved, yet extremely winning manners. They have both been teachers in the public schools for several sessions and Miss Eva is also quite a talented musician. Messrs. Fike and Davis are citizens of Hattiesburg and are both prominent young business men of that place. The News wishes for them every happiness that life can bring. *The Perry County News,* April 11, 1919, Vol. VIII, No. 20

Miss Minnie Mixon of this place and Mr. Benjamin Prestidge, of Jacksonville, Fla., were married last Saturday evening at the Parsonage of the Main St. Methodist church, in Hattiesburg, the Rev. Paul D. Hardin officiating. Miss Mixon has been in Hattiesburg for the past year but is well known here and has many friends who extend their best wishes for a happy wedded life.
The Perry County News, April 11, 1919, Vol. VIII, No. 20

Little Jim Wash Irby, Jr., the two year old son of Mr. and Mrs. J. W. Irby, died at the family residence at Old Augusta last Saturday night after an illness of seven weeks, from a complication of diseases. The little body was laid to rest Sunday afternoon in the Old Augusta cemetery.
The Perry County News, April 18, 1919, Vol. VIII, No. 21

The friends of Miss Edna Mathis of Beaumont will be interested in learning of her recent marriage to a Mr. Carroll, of Mobile. Miss Edna has made many friends among the young people here during her visits to her aunt, Mrs. H. P. Smith, all of whom wish for her the greatest amount of happiness. *The Perry County News,* April 18, 1919, Vol. VIII, No. 21

Little Robert Fitzhugh George died Tuesday night at the home of his grandmother, Mrs. S. E. McCoy, after an illness of ten days from colitis. Mrs. George, with the two children, had been visiting her mother only a week when the little fellow became ill, but his condition was not thought critical until Monday afternoon. At that time his symptoms became so alarming that a message was sent for his father, who arrived Tuesday morning. Every effort possible to give relief and check the disease was made by physician and family but God had beckoned and the little one grew steadily worse until the end, when he quietly and peacefully went to sleep. Little Robert Fitz was just seventeen months old and was a winsome and lovable child. His merry baby laughter had an irresistible way of twining itself around ones heartstrings, and his going will leave an aching void in the hearts of the stricken parents and loved ones which only time can heal. Funeral services were held at the residence at 3:30 o'clock Wednesday afternoon, conducted by Rev. J. N. McMillin, and interment was made in the Old Augusta cemetery. *The Perry County News,* April 25, 1919, Vol. VIII, No. 22

Twin baby boys came to the home of Mr. and Mrs. S. J. Maxwell Wednesday morning but they lived only a short time and both little bodies were buried in the Old Augusta cemetery Wednesday afternoon. *The Perry County News,* May 9, 1919, Vol. VIII, No. 24

God's plans work in a mysterious way His wonders to perform. No knows why Joe Wright was protected by the guiding spirit of the God of love through the battle's roar and hell's shot and shell and spared to again lovingly embrace his mother and give his friends that hearty handshake which only Joe knew how to give. Yet the life of the hero that he was was spared and when he arrived in the states looking fine, hearty and healthy no one could afford to believe that he would so soon meet an untimely death in a saw mill accident at Lyman, Miss. On Friday morning at 8 o'clock, May 9, 1919, Joe died as he had lived---a hero at the helm. In the twinkling of an eye his life went out to the great beyond. Joe Austin Wright was born at Meridian, Miss., Nov. 25, 1896, reared at New Augusta, was a son of Mrs. Ora Dennis, of Wingate and Jesse Austin Wright, deceased. He joined the M. E. Church South in his early days and lived an upright Christian life. Joined the U. S. Army on July 4, 1916, when Uncle Sam called for heroes, and ever displayed that greatness of heroic spirit of an American soldier. Corporal Joe Austin Wright was a member of Co. C, of the fighting 155th Infantry, was on the Mexican border, trained at Beauregard, La., went overseas in June 1918, was on the front in France, returned and received his discharge from the Army in Feb. 1919 with all the honors due and becoming a patriotic and faithful soldier. With all the possibilities of a long, happy and prosperous life before him he was cut down like a tender rosebud to wither and decay; but its fragrance will ever live in the hearts and minds of his friends and loved ones. Joe leaves to mourn his loss his mother, Mrs. Ora Dennis, of Wingate, stepfather, W. A. Dennis, a brother, Harry Wright, of the Rainbow Division, a sister, Mrs. Alberta Harrison, of Gulfport, Miss., many comrades who served with him in the Army and many other relatives and friends. *The Perry County News,* May 16, 1919, Vol. VIII, No. 25

Johnson E. Hinton and Miss Edna Easterling were married last Saturday afternoon at the home of the bride's parents, near Hattiesburg, Rev. E. Bruce officiating. They will reside at the Hinton home here, a few miles north of town. The News extends congratulations.
The Perry County News, May 23, 1919, Vol. VIII, No. 26

Mr. A. U. (Uncle Abner) Carter died at his home a few miles north of town last Saturday at 11 o'clock a.m. after an illness of several days. Mr. Carter was a hustling, progressive farmer, one of the best citizens of the country, and a man whose place it will be hard to fill. He leaves a large family and many relatives to mourn his loss.
The Perry County News, May 23, 1919, Vol. VIII, No. 26

A marriage of considerable interest here was that last Saturday afternoon of Forrest H. Cochran and Miss Iona Cooper. The wedding took place at the home of the bride's parents in the Deep Creek community. Forrest's home is out in the Agness neighborhood but he was an employee of Kennedy Bros. Here for many months, so we feel that he is one of our boys. He has only recently returned from the shipyards at Pascagoula and Moss Point where he worked for about a year. His bride has been an efficient teacher in the Deep Creek School for some time. Both are fine young people and the News joins the many friends in wishing them every success in life.
The Perry County News, May 23, 1919, Vol. VIII, No. 26

Cupid could never be arraigned for vagrancy! Everybody thought he was just taking a much needed rest from his double duty of last week, when to the surprise of most everyone last Sunday he perfected a job which culminated in the marriage of Mr. Forrest E. Davis to Miss Raidee Dunkley, both of Wingate. The wedding took place at the home of the bride's parents, at that place, Rev. J. N. McMillin officiating. Forrest is the oldest son of Mrs. F. F. Hinton and is a young man of sterling worth. For several months he was in the U. S. Navy, only recently being discharged from service. Miss Raidee is a girl of most lovable qualities and is a general favorite among the younger set. The News wishes and predicts for the young couple a happy and prosperous life. *The Perry County News,* May 30, 1919, Vol. VIII, No. 27

A beautiful little daughter arrived Tuesday morning at the home of Prof. and Mrs. W. H. Robinson. *The Perry County News,* June 6, 1919, Vol. VIII, No. 28

Mr. B. F. Garraway, familiarly known as "Uncle Ben", who for several months has made his home with his brother, J. P. Garraway, neared Mahned, died at 11 0'clock Wednesday morning, after an illness of two weeks. Uncle Ben was about 78 years of age and has been a resident of this section of the country for many years and was very prominently connected. He was a man of exceptional character and his passing is a distinct loss to our country. He leaves many relatives to mourn his death to which the News extends its deepest sympathy.
The Perry County News, July 18, 1919, Vol. VIII, No. 34

Last Sunday morning while the residents of our little community went to church for their hour of worship the spirit of Mrs. Rosebella McSwain winged its way to the Church on High to continue the eternal praise and worship begun on earth many years ago. For about eighteen months Mrs. McSwain had been in failing health and for the past five months had been confined to her room and bed almost continuously. Last Wednesday night her condition became much worse and for three days before her death was almost hourly expected. All her life, prior to her last illness, she had been unusually strong and robust, so her months of confinement were a great trial to her whose life had been as full of activity as had hers, but in all her suffering, which at times was intense, never was she heard to murmur against the providence which had brought her from a life of useful and unceasing work to that of a helpless invalid. In her death we have lost one from the church and community whose place it will be hard to fill and a place is left vacant in the home which can never be filled except as the sad, sweet memory of her beautiful life flows into the bruised and bleeding hearts of the loved ones left behind. All who knew Mrs. McSwain knew her for what she was a pure, conscientious Christian and a kind, sympathetic, and helpful neighbor and friend. Possibly no hands have ever ministered to the suffering and needy of her community more than hers; possibly no lips have spoken more words of sympathy and comfort to those in sorrow and distress; no Christian has been more zealous and faithful in her church than she; and certain it is that no soul has gone to a sweeter or richer reward had she lived till next month she would have been 67 years of age. She was a daughter of James B. and Ellen Ulman; married in 1872 to Colin M. McSwain, who preceded her to the grave fifteen years. To this union were born ten children, seven of whom are living, all being at her bedside when the end came. She was the grandmother of fourteen children. Her funeral was held at the Methodist Church, of which she was a member for forty years, conducted by the pastor, Rev. J. C. Ellis. The pallbearers were D. B. Griffin, C. C. Dearman, J. A. Kennedy, Fitz L. McCoy, J. Oliver, and J. F. Ruffin. Following the funeral, interment was made in the family cemetery one mile north of town. The many beautiful floral offerings bore mute testimony of her popularity in the community. We would point the sorrowing loved ones to Him who doeth all things well. He alone can wipe their tears away and heal the wounds of a rendered heart.

The Perry County News, August 22, 1919, Vol. VIII, No. 39

Births, Deaths, and Marriages

1921 - 1930

Through an oversight last week, we failed to mention the arrivals of two wee young ladies recently, one to the home of Mr. and Mrs. W. B. Mills and the other to the home of Mr. and Mrs. A. E. Hinton. *The Perry County News,* January 27, 1922, Vol. VV, No. 40

Mr. Leslie Webb and Miss Floy Watkins stole a march on their friends last Saturday afternoon and were quietly married at the bride's home. They left immediately for a short trip to the Gulf Coast after which they went to Avera, where they will reside. Miss Floy is the eldest daughter of Mr. and Mrs. A. T. L. Watkins, and is a young lady of sterling worth---well fitted to reign as queen in the home of her chosen companion. Mr. Webb has for a good many years been a resident of Greene County and is a hustling young business man. The News wishes this estimable couple all possible joy in their wedded life.
The Perry County News, February 10, 1922, Vol. VV, No. 42

Mr. Lewis Posey and Miss Grace Anderson, both living down toward the Agness community were married Wednesday morning at the courthouse by Justice J. W. Thomas. Both these young people are well known and are very popular in their community and their many friends wish for them a happy life together. *The Perry County News,* February 17, 1922, Vol. VV, No. 43

The two year old daughter of Mr. and Mrs. Peter Fairley died Wednesday morning at the family residence at Wingate, following a two week illness of pneumonia. Burial was had Thursday morning in the new cemetery, Rev. J. C. Ellis officiating.
The Perry County News, March 3, 1922, Vol. VV, No. 45

Herman, the fifteen months old baby of Mr. and Mrs. E. L. Story, of Mahned, died early Monday morning after ten days illness of pneumonia proceeded by whooping cough. As we went to press last week the little one was reported to be much better and it was thought he would get well, but the poison from the disease had been so absorbed by the system that, in his frail condition he had not the vital force to combat it. Burial was made in the Mahned cemetery, where another baby of this couple, their first born is buried. *The Perry County News,* March 17, 1922, Vol. VV, No. 47

A marriage of much interest to people here was that of Mr. C. E. Wilson, cashier of the bank at this place, and Miss Bessie Denham, of Hattiesburg, which took place last evening (Thursday) at the home of the bride's parents, Mr. and Mrs. H. W. Denham. The event was a quiet home affair, only the relatives and a few close personal friends witnessing the ceremony, which was performed at 9:30 o'clock by the Rev. W. F. Yarbrough, pastor of First Baptist Church at that place. The bride is a member of one of this country's pioneer families, being a granddaughter of Capt. J. W. Denham, of Mahned, one of the most highly esteemed citizens this county has ever had, and is a young woman of rare accomplishments. She possesses a lovely voice and figures prominently in all musical numbers given by the younger set of her home town. Mr. Wilson came here in February to take charge of the affairs of the Bank and has made himself immensely popular with everyone in our community.

The young couple left immediately following the ceremony for a short trip to Birmingham. Upon their return they will, for the present, be domiciled with Mr. and Mrs. H. C. Hughes of this place, the latter being the bride's aunt. The News joins their friends in hearty congratulations and a cordial welcome to our town. *The Perry County News,* April 7, 1922, Vol. VV, No. 50

Newell Chase Boungton, Jr. is the very big name given to the very little son who arrived at the home of his parents on Saturday, May 27. *The Perry County News,* June 2, 1922, Vol. VVI, No. 6

Mrs. C. T. Rawls, an aged woman living near Agnes, died yesterday afternoon and was buried today in the New Augusta Cemetery. *The Perry County News,* July 14, 1922, Vol. VVI, No. 12

Just as we go to press we learn of the death of Mrs. J. J. Stevens, which occurred early this morning at her home in Hattiesburg. She is well known here, being the widow of Dr. J. J. Stevens, who spent several months here prior to his death. Funeral services will be held in Hattiesburg Saturday at eleven o'clock.
The Perry County News, August 18, 1922, Vol. VVI, No. 17

We regret very much to note the death of R. H. Jones of Columbia, who passed away in the hospital there after four weeks from Typhoid fever. Mr. Jones was a former resident of Mahned and later lived for some time down on the "Central" when the Newman works were first established. He was a man of sterling qualities and of strong convictions and he was a citizen who will be greatly missed in his community. He leaves a widow and several children, among them Mrs. D. D. Hairston, of this place, and Mrs. E. L. Story, of Mahned, both of whom were with him when the end came. Interment took place in the Mahned cemetery Thursday of last week, the funeral service being conducted by Rev. J. C. Ellis. The News extends sympathy to the bereaved ones. *The Perry County News,* August 18, 1922, Vol. VVI, No. 17

Died at the family home in Beaumont, Perry County, Mississippi, on Tuesday, August 8, 1922, Mr. J. L. Daughdrill, after being bed-ridden for some nine months. Jack had a tubercular trouble and has been a great suffer for this long time. He was a man of gentle temperament and had a happy faculty of being friendly with pretty near everbody. His remains were brought to Greene County and buried in the Daughdrill graveyard near benco station. He was the oldest son of W. T. Daughdrill and a brother to Kim Daughdrill and others. He was 42 years old. Jack leaves a wife and three children and they have a very good farm place up there in Perry County and a good crop growing on it this year. The oldest son is 15 years old and looks after the crop. (Greene County Herald) *The Perry County News,* August 25, 1922, Vol. VVI, No. 18

The many friends will be interested in learning of the birth of a daughter to Mr. and Mrs. T. S. Jackson, of Hattiesburg. Mrs. Jackson was formerly Miss Telula McMillin, daughter of Dr. J. N. McMillin, pastor of the Baptist Church here. She was a member of the school faculty here several years ago. *The Perry County News,* September 15, 1922, Vol. VVI, No. 21

Dr. E. S. P'Pool who had been ill for several weeks, died here at any early hour Thursday morning. His body was embalmed and carried to Hattiesburg to await the arrival of some of his children who were far away, and later to be carried to Learned to rest in the old family cemetery. *The Perry County News,* September 22, 1922, Vol. VVI, No. 22

We regret very much to chronicle the death of Mr. L. S. McCoy, of Beaumont, who passed away at his home here Wednesday of this week, following several days illness from apoplexy. Mr. McCoy was a well-known figure here and belonged to one of Perry County's most prominent families. Interment took place at Beaumont Thursday afternoon and a great many from this place attended the funeral. *The Perry County News,* November 24, 1922, Vol. VVI, No. 31

A little son was born Wednesday to Mr. and Mrs. Leslie Webb at the home of the grandparents, Mr. and Mrs. A. T. L. Watkins. *The Perry County News,* January 5, 1923, Vol. VVI, No. 37

New Augusta has two new citizens since our last issue-the little son who came to the home of Mr. and Mrs. N. W. Carpenter on the evening of Jan. 5th and the wee daughter who arrived at the home of W. W. Dennis and wife on January 9th. *The Perry County News,* January 12, 1923, Vol. VVI, No. 38

Willie Burt Rainer is the name of the little son who came to make his home with Mr. and Mrs. J. E. Rainer, Jr. *The Perry County News,* January 12, 1923, Vol. VVI, No. 38

We regret very much to chronicle the death of Mr. L. S. McCoy of Beaumont, who passed away at his home here Wednesday of this week following several days of illness from apoplexy. Mr. McCoy was a well-known figure here and belonged to one of Perry County's most prominent families. Interment took place at Beaumont Thursday afternoon and a great many from this place attended the funeral. *The Perry County News,* February 2, 1923, Vol. VVI, No. 41

Sam Cooley, whose home was down in the Janice Community, died of flu Wednesday evening and was buried Thursday. *The Perry County News,* February 9, 1923, Vol. VVI, No. 42

Born to Mr. and Mrs. B. W. Smith on February 24, a girl. *The Perry County News,* March 2, 1923, Vol. VVI, No. 45

New Augusta has two new citizens since our last publication. A wee lassie came to the home of Mr. and Mrs. M. D. Fullilove last Saturday, and on the following Monday a tiny lad was added to the family of Mr. and Mrs. C. C. Dearman. *The Perry County News,* March 23, 1923, Vol. VVI, No. 48

Attorney Harmon D. Young, of this place, was married to Miss Adelia Olander at Louisville, Ky. Last Sunday morning. While the approaching event was known to a few close friends of the parties, it came as a complete surprise to most of New Augusta folks. Miss Olander was a member of the school faculty here a few years ago, and won many friends during her stay among us. She is a young woman of most winning personality, and rare accomplishments. Everyone knows Mr. Young. He came here some ten years ago, and began the practice of law.

Enlisted with Uncle Sam's fighting men and did duty with the A. E. F. in France for several months, upon his return taking up his law practice again. The newly wedded couple returned Wednesday and will make their home here. The News joins their many friends in wishing them many happy and prosperous years. *The Perry County News,* March 23, 1923, Vol. VVI, No. 48

A little son was born last Friday night to Mr. and Mrs. A. J. Lutz, but God, in His infinite wisdom, saw fit to recall the little life early Monday morning. Funeral services were held Tuesday morning at the home by Rev. D. P. McIntosh, pastor of the Presbyterian Church here, following which the tiny body was laid to rest in the Old Augusta cemetery, beside another baby of the family, which passed on a few years ago.
The Perry County News, April 6, 1923, Vol. VVI, No. 50

David H., Jr. is the name given to the little son that arrived at the home of Mr. and Mrs. D. H. Horn out on Route 1, Saturday, April 21.
The Perry County News, April 27, 1923, Vol. VVII, No. 1

It is with sincere regret that we note the death of Sheppard M. Hinton which occurred in a hospital in Hattiesburg last Monday morning. He had been operated upon for appendicitis about one week before and had been critically ill from the first. He was buried at the old farm home near Benmore, Tuesday, Rev. S. T. Courtney conducting the funeral service. An immense crowd of relatives attended. The death of this young man, whose life gave promise of such splendid success and accomplishment, came as a shock to his many friends throughout the county. He was in the race for Circuit and Chancery Clerk, and his announcement was being carried in this paper. *The Perry County News,* May 4, 1923, Vol. VVII, No. 2

Miss Annie Thompson and N. C. Smith were married last Sunday.
The Perry County News, June 1, 1923, Vol. VVII, No. 6

Friends will be interested to learn of the tiny daughter of Mr. and Mrs. A. E. Davis, at Sanford. The mother will be remembered as Miss Eva McDonald.
The Perry County News, June 8, 1923, Vol. VVII, No. 7

Fitz L. McCoy left Tuesday for Lake, where he and Miss Marbeth Freeman were married yesterday. They expect to be at home here within the next few days. A more complete write up of the marriage will appear in the next issue of the paper.
The Perry County News, June 8, 1923, Vol. VVII, No. 7

Friends of the family deeply sympathize with J. G. Tucker in the sudden death of his mother, which occurred at his home a few miles south of town Wednesday afternoon. She had been in rather frail health for some time but her condition was not known to be so serious and her death comes as a shock to her family and friends.
The Perry County News, June 15, 1923, Vol. VVII, No. 8

An out of town wedding that will be of unusual interest to the people of this community was that of Miss Marbeth Freeman, daughter of Mr. and Mrs. J. A. Freeman of Lake, and Mr. Fitzhugh L. McCoy of New Augusta. The wedding was solemnized in the First Baptist Church of Lake, at 12 O'Clock on Thursday, June 7, 1923, before an interested gathering of friends and well-wishers. The bride was given away by her father, Mr. J. A. Freeman. The groom's best man was Dewey S. Dearman of New Augusta. Immediately after the ceremony the newly-weds left for New Orleans, which city they spent a few days before going to New Augusta, where they are at home with Mrs. Pearl Cadenhead of this place.
The Perry County News, June 15, 1923, Vol. VVII, No. 8

This entire community was shocked yesterday afternoon when a message came from Hattiesburg announcing the death of D. K. McDonald which had just occurred there in the Infirmary. We understand that Mr. McDonald was seized with an attack of acute indigestion last Tuesday and taken to the above named institution for treatment but his condition did not appear serious until a few hours before his death. He was buried in Old Augusta cemetery Friday afternoon, an immense crowd of friends and relatives present. The funeral service was conducted by Dr. J. N. McMillin, assisted by Dr. W. F. Yarbrough.
The Perry County News, July 6, 1923, Vol. VVII, No. 11

The funeral services for the infant son which was born last Friday to Mr. and Mrs. H. B. Hinton were held at the home Saturday after which burial was made in the family cemetery. Friends of the family deeply sympathize with them in the loss of their new born baby and that sympathy is even more from the fact that only a week prior to this, Mr. Hinton lost his mother.
The Perry County News, August 31, 1923, Vol. VVII, No. 19

Friends of Mr. and Mrs. C. E. Wilson will be interested in knowing of the little daughter who came to them last Tuesday at the South Mississippi Infirmary in Hattiesburg.
The Perry County News, August 31, 1923, Vol. VVII, No. 19

A quiet home wedding but one of much interest to the many friends of the family was that of Miss Minnie Smith of this place and Mr. G. T. Parrot, of Flippin, Ark., which was solemnized at the home of the bride's mother last Sunday morning, Rev. Hilary S. Westbrook, Methodist pastor, officiating. The happy pair left immediately for their home in the neighbor state. The News joins their many friends in wishing them success and happiness.
The Perry County News, August 31, 1923, Vol. VVII, No.19

Mr. C. C. Garrison, of Mahned, and Miss Gertrude Thompson, of Alabama, were united in marriage last Sunday afternoon at the home of the groom, Justice C. E. White officiating.
The Perry County News, September 7, 1923, Vol. VVII, No. 20

A. A. Dinkins, of Richton, and Miss Estelle Maples, of Leaksville, were married at the Methodist Parsonage here last Saturday, Rev. Hilary S. Westbrook officiating.
The Perry County News, September 14, 1923, Vol. VVII, No. 21

Our entire community was saddened last Friday evening when the word was passed from one to another that Cam Watkins was dead. He had been suffering for several months with a serious affection of the mouth and throat, but his condition was not recognized by his family and friends as being so serious until a few days before his death. His suffering was intense, but he bore it bravely, and his physician and loved ones were untiring in their efforts to alleviate his pain. He lost all consciousness two or three days before his death and never regained it, but the end came quietly and with perfect ease. Cam had lived here since he was a mere lad, had grown up to manhood with the boys and girls of the town, and was popular with all. He had joined the Methodist Church a good many years ago, and he lived a clean, Christian life. He was one of ten children of Mr. and Mrs. A. T. L. Watkins. Cam will be sadly missed by his family, his friends and his community. But when "He who doeth all things well" called, there was nothing left to do but answer the summons. *The Perry County News,* September 28, 1923, Vol. VVII, No. 23

Mr. Otis Shattles of Brooklyn and Miss Minnie Bell of Wingate were married at the courthouse here last Saturday afternoon by Justice C. E. White. The affair was a complete surprise to their many friends and no one knew of the approaching event until it was over. Mr. Shattles is a prominent businessman of the old Janice community while his bride is one of the most popular young ladies of this community as well as her own. She has done professional nursing in this section of the country for several years. Her friends regret that her marriage will take her elsewhere to live, but are unanimous in wishing the couple every success in life.
The Perry County News, October 23, 1923, Vol. VVII, No. 26

Death always brings sorrow, heartache, and tears of anguish but when it ruthlessly fells two loved ones in the home within a week it is doubly sad. Such is the case in the home of Mrs. E. R. Anderson, who lives about seven miles south of town. Last Saturday morning a son, Enoch, died after ten days illness with pneumonia, and Tuesday morning of this week the husband and father of the home, Elisha R. Anderson, succumbed to an illness of several months duration. He was confined to his bed, however, less than one week. Both bodies were laid to rest in the family cemetery near the home. The Anderson family is one of the most prominent in their community, and these two good men will be sadly missed. Rev. M. W. Matthews conducted the funeral services of the son, while that of Mr. Anderson was held by Dr. L. G. Gates, who is conducting a meeting at the Baptist Church here this week. The News extends its sincere sympathy to the bereaved family. *The Perry County News,* October 23, 1923, Vol. VVII, No. 26

As the sad news spread over the Pearce's creek community from friend to friend of the death of Mrs. Mary Hogan I can hear them saying "Another good woman gone to her reward." After an illness of pneumonia for six days, she passed quietly away on Monday afternoon, November 12, at 3:30 o'clock. She was the devoted wife of W. M. Hogan and the loving mother of two children, Mrs. Alice Martin and Miss Ollie Hogan. She leaves her mother, Mrs. Jane Mixon, one sister, Mrs. Mattie McCardle, and two brothers, Bob and Mark Mixon. She had been a member of the Baptist church here for twelve years, and was a consecrated Christian woman, a kind and loving friend and neighbor.

What higher praise can be given her memory? Her body was laid to rest in the family cemetery nearby, on Tuesday afternoon at 3 o'clock. The funeral service was conducted by Rev. D. A. Hogan, of Hattiesburg, her former pastor. To the husband and motherless children this entire community extends sincere sympathy. A. Friend
The Perry County News, November 23, 1923, Vol. VVII, No. 31

Thanksgiving Day was made more beautiful, more joyous, and more impressive by the marriage of Mr. Dewey C. Morris and Miss Audrey Myers, which was solemnized at nine o'clock yesterday morning. It was a quiet home affair, beautiful in its simplicity, where the very atmosphere breathed love, and peace, and happiness. The house had been beautifully and artistically decorated with gold ribbons and autumn foliage, the same color scheme having been used in all the pre-nuptial social events. The dining room, thru which the bridal couple approached, had the path enclosed with ribbons of gold, these ribbons still marking the way to the living room, where, beneath a beautiful canopy of gold and autumn leaves, from which the soft light shed a subdued radiance about them, and just in front of a magnificent embankment of ferns and autumn boughs, the happy pair took the vows so old, so new, which united them, "Two souls with but a single thought, two hearts that beat as one." Rev. D. P. McIntosh, pastor of the Presbyterian Church, officiated, the double ring ceremony being used, just prior to which Mrs. C. E. Wilson sang, in her beautiful soprano, "At Dawning." She was accompanied on the piano by Mrs. Eugene Terry, who also played the nuptial marches and, throughout the ceremony played very softly, the "Minuet in G." Mr. Morris is a young man of unquestioned character, a native son of Perry County, having been reared at Morristown, (the community getting its name from the Morris family) which was originally in this county. He is the son of the late F. M. Morris, one of the most prominent and best loved citizens of Forrest and Perry counties. Being a graduate of the A & M College, he is now the efficient teacher of agriculture in the A. H. S. at Brooklyn, Forrest County, now serving his second year in that capacity. The bride is one of New Augusta's loveliest and most popular girls. She has been for the past few years the very efficient clerk in the Perry County Bank, having accepted that position as soon as she finished school. It is a well-recognized fact that her ready smile and cheerful service made many friends and patrons for that institution. She possesses the charm and personality which so peculiarly fits her for the sphere of a help meet and homemaker for the man of her choice. She is the youngest daughter of Mrs. Belle Myers, one of the finest and best loved women of this place. Immediately following the ceremony, the happy couple, amid a shower of rice and good wishes, left for a short honeymoon trip to the coast, after which they will be at home at Brooklyn. The News extends to them the sincere wish that their married life may be long and useful and be all that they wish it to be, and when, eventually, that life shall close it may end still encircled with the halo of its beginning. *The Perry County News,* November 30, 1923, Vol. VVII, No. 32

Every citizen of New Augusta was shocked and saddened last Saturday morning when the news was passed around that Mrs. Barbara McInnis was dead. The end came very suddenly at the home of her brother, Judge J. H. Davis, with whom she has made her home since the death of his wife some four years ago. She arose as usual that morning and went to the kitchen to prepare the morning meal. A few minutes later she was found dead, seated in her rocking chair on the back porch, outside the kitchen door, her countenance as calm and peaceful as that of a child asleep. Death had evidently come without a struggle or a murmur. She had been somewhat indisposed for several days with a cold but was apparently in her usual health when she retired Friday night.

Her physician pronounced her death due to heart failure. "Aunt Barbara" as she was lovingly called by all who knew her, had lived here for the past five years, and not a man, woman, or child but knew and loved her tender smile and gentle manner. Her husband preceded her to the grave more than thirty years ago. They had no children, but she was too busy doing good to others to live a lonely life. She professed Christianity and joined the Presbyterian Church when quite young, and, as her pastor Rev. D. P. McIntosh, so beautifully and fittingly said, "she grew in grace until God saw it was enough and called her home to enter into her eternal reward." The tear dimmed eyes, the aching hearts, the heart broken sobs, the magnificent floral offerings, were all testimonies of the esteem in which she was held, and of the grief her going left behind. The funeral service was held in the Presbyterian Church Sunday morning at 11 o'clock, the body was then followed by a large concourse of friends to the cemetery where it was laid, by tender hands, in its final resting place. Her immediate relatives left are her brother, J. H. Davis, of this place, and Mrs. Mary M. Barnes, of Lumberton, a number of nieces and nephews, and many more distant relatives. *The Perry County News,* December 7, 1923, Vol. VVII, No. 33

The funeral services of Colon Andrew McSwain were conducted here on last Friday, November 20th. Mr. McSwain died in New Orleans Thursday, November 19th and his remains were brought here for burial in the family cemetery on the old homestead just north of New Augusta. Colon, as he was familiarly known, was born December 17th, 1881. He grew up to manhood in this vicinity and spent many of his young manhood here among us. He graduated from the University of Mississippi Law School a number of years ago and practiced his profession in the courts of this and adjoining counties. He later removed to Oklahoma City, Okla., and was practicing his profession there at the time this last illness came upon him. Mr. McSwain is survived by his wife and small daughter and three brothers and three sisters, Mrs. B.T. Robinson and A. A. McSwain of New Augusta; R.G. McSwain, Red Gum, La.; U. C. McSwain, Canton, Miss.; Miss Mamie McSwain, New Orleans, and Mrs. M. J. Irban {Urban}, of Columbia, Miss. The funeral services were held at the Methodist Church and were conducted by Rev. Neil McIntosh and Rev. J. C. Ellis. We extend our sympathy to the bereaved wife and other members of the family. *The Richton Dispatch,* November 27, 1925, Vol. XX, No. 18

Mrs. J. M. Schillings, born and reared near Old Augusta, member of the Methodist church of New Augusta died April 5, 10 a.m. in the home of her brother, Mr. Bruce McSwain, of Old Augusta. The funeral was conducted in the home of her brother at 10 o'clock Tuesday by her Pastor Rev. J. C. Jackson assisted by her former Pastor Rev. J. C. Ellis, after which she was buried in the Old Augusta cemetery by the side of her only son and child who was buried there about fifteen years ago. Her husband died and was buried in Georgia about ten years ago. A large concourse of sympathizing relatives and friends attended the funeral services and burial. *The Richton Dispatch,* April 9, 1926, Vol. XX, No. 37

The following out-of-town people were present at the funeral of little Eran McSwain Garraway, infant daughter of Mr. and Mrs. H. P. Garraway born Monday night the 10th, and died Tuesday morning, the 11th, was buried in the New Augusta cemetery Wednesday morning: Mrs. Dewey Wilder, of Hattiesburg; Mr. J. L. Miller, of Columbia, and Mr. and Mrs. Smith Garraway, of Hattiesburg. *The Richton Dispatch,* May 14, 1926, Vol. XX, No. 42

Mr. Malcolm McKenzie, of near McCallum, fell dead Monday morning, June 7th, in the lot at his house. He was buried Tuesday at 10 o'clock in the family cemetery.
The Richton Dispatch, June 18, 1926, Vol. XX, No. 47

Mr. Earl McSwain, a young man 32 years of age, suffered sunstroke last Saturday, which resulted in his death Sunday evening at five o'clock in Service, Ala. His body was brought to New Augusta Methodist Church in the early morning hours of Tuesday, where his funeral was preached at nine a.m. by Revs. J. C. Jackson and J. G. Ellis. Quite a crowd of friends and relatives were present. Among the relatives were also his sister and her husband, Mr. and Mrs. Clem Harris, of Montgomery, Ala. The body was carried to the Old Augusta cemetery for interment. The floral offering was very pretty. One brother, Mr. Webster McSwain failed to arrive for the funeral. *The Richton Dispatch,* August 27, 1926, Vol. XXI, No. 5

Births, Deaths, and Marriages

1931 - 1941

This entire community was shocked at the sudden and tragic death of Adolph Gillis, 38, who lived about 5 miles from here and a brother of Mrs. Harvey Myers of this place. The funeral was held Tuesday afternoon at the family residence with the Rev. Blackwelder of Petal and Pastor of the Presbyterian Church here, and Rev. Will McIntosh of Hattiesburg, officiating interment was in the family cemetery near the old McKenzie place, the former home of Mrs. Gillis. He is survived by his widow; Mrs. Kate McKenzie Gillis, three daughters Raybeth, Willie Mae and Gladis; mother, Mrs. Lizzie Gillis, all of New Augusta; two brothers, Buford Gillis of New Augusta and Homer Gillis of Hattiesburg, two sisters, Mrs. Edna Stevens of Prospect Community and Mrs. Harvey Myers of this place.
The Richton Dispatch, January 20, 1933, Vol. XXVII, No. 27

The many friends here of Mr. Albert Allen McSwain of Hintonville Community regretted very much to learn of his death which occurred at his home last Tuesday. Mr. McSwain had been in very poor health for the past year or two but his death was quite sudden. He grew worse last Monday night and passed away the following day. Funeral and interment was at the S. L. Hinton cemetery on Wednesday. We extend our deepest sympathy to the family in their bereavement.
The Richton Dispatch, February 3, 1933, Vol. XXVII, No. 29

Funeral services for Bernard McSwain, 28, who died at the South Miss. Infirmary last week following a short illness of acute sinus, with complications was held here last Thursday afternoon at 3 o'clock in the Methodist church with a host of relatives and friends present to mourn his going. The Rev. E. M. Allen, Pastor of this church of which Bernard had been a member since early childhood, was in charge of the service. The deceased was the second oldest son of Mr. and Mrs. A. A. McSwain. He was born here and spent almost all of his life here, except 3 years spent in the service of his country. Bernard was a very likable boy, and numbered his friends by his acquaintances. Although quiet and retiring by nature he was very popular and to know him was to love him. Pallbearers were: C. S. Myers, J. C. McDonald, Jr., Cecil Hammett, Ernest McCoy, Jr., Edwin Allen, John B. Dennis and Charlie Smith. Interment was in the New Augusta cemetery. Bernard is survived by his parents, Mr. and Mrs. A. A. McSwain; one sister, Mrs. A. C. Matthews; five brothers, David, Aubrey, Clifford, Wilfred and Elliot, all of New Augusta and Russell McSwain of New Orleans.
The Richton Dispatch, February 3, 1933, Vol. XXVII, No. 29

A wedding of much interest to Richton people is that of one of the young men, who has grown up here and is well known in the surrounding community as well and that is Shirley Jacobs, who took as his bride, Miss Ireda Daniel, of D'Lo. The wedding occurred in Hattiesburg on November 2 with Rev. R. E. Massey, officiating. Best wishes of Shirley's friends are extended them. *The Richton Dispatch,* November 13, 1936, Vol. XXXI, No. 18

This community was saddened and shocked Thursday to learn of the sudden death of Reuben D. Breland, of New Orleans, second son of Mr. and Mrs. G. Y. Breland of Kittrell. The body arrived here Friday and was laid to rest Saturday morning in the family cemetery.
The Richton Dispatch, November 20, 1936, Vol. XXXI, No. 19

Mr. and Mrs. Walter Henbest are the happy parents of a fine baby boy born on Nov. 15 and has been named Walter Glen Henbest, Jr. Mr. Henbest is Farm Supt. Of the Emery Memorial Home and Mrs. Henbest is secretary there.
The Richton Dispatch, November 27, 1936, Vol. XXXI, No. 20

Burial rites for John Franklin Mixon, 80, pioneer resident of New Augusta, was held Tuesday morning at 10 o'clock at the Indian Springs Church with the Rev. E. M. Bilbo officiating. Interment was in the church cemetery. Mr. Mixon, a farmer of Perry county, had been in failing health for some time. He is survived by five daughters: Mrs. B. T. Prestridge, Mrs. T. J. Eure, Miss Margaret Mixon, all of Hattiesburg, Mrs. Alice James of Poplarville, and Mrs. H. E. Morren of New Augusta, and two sons, T. D. Mixon of Runnelstown and B. F. Mixon, Alsatia, La. He is also survived by 21 grandchildren and 11 great-grandchildren.
The Richton Dispatch, November 27, 1936, Vol. XXXI, No. 20

A wedding that was quietly solemnized on Thanksgiving afternoon which was of interest in Richton and surrounding community, joined Arthur Caldwell and Miss Dorothy Walley as man and wife. The ceremony was performed in the home of Mrs. M. V. Caldwell, mother of the groom, Rev. V. W. Malley officiating. The bride, an attractive brunette, is the only daughter of Mr. and Mrs. Laurence Walley and has made her home in Richton since childhood. She finished Richton High School and later attended Junior College at Ellisville. "Buddie," as the groom is affectionately known to the boys and girls here, is the only son of Mrs. M. V. Caldwell and came to Richton when just a small boy, formerly having made his home in Ellisville. After finishing high school in Richton he attended Junior College at Ellisville from which he graduated and since that time has taught in the public school here and served as assistant coach. He has also attended S. T. C. for two summer sessions. Best wishes are being extended the happy young couple by their many friends. *The Richton Dispatch,* December 4, 1936, Vol. XXXI, No. 21

A very sad occasion occurred at Pleasant Hill community Monday when the death angel came to the home of Mr. Zollie Byrd and called to her heavenly reward his wife, Mrs. Roxana Brewer Byrd. She leaves her companion, 10 children, a father, 6 sisters, 4 brothers and a host of relatives and friends to mourn her departure. Her body was laid in the family cemetery to await the Resurrection Day. The funeral was in charge of Wright & Freeman Undertaking Co. The services being conducted by the Pastor Luther K. Turner.
The Richton Dispatch, December 4, 1936, Vol. XXXI, No. 21

Miss Bernice Hinton and Mr. Terry Hurst were married in Hattiesburg, Nov. 28, 1936. The Reverend Thomas F. Harvey, pastor of the First Baptist Church performing the ceremony. Mrs. Hurst is the only child of Mr. and Mrs. S. L. Hinton, Jr. of New Augusta. Mr. Hurst is the son of Mr. and Mrs. Thomas Hurst of Hattiesburg. After the ceremony the couple left for a short trip to the coast, on their return they will be at home at 809 James St., Hattiesburg.
The Richton Dispatch, December 11, 1936, Vol. XXXI, No. 22

Everyone was very much surprised to hear about the wedding of Miss V. Harrison to Mr. Clinton Anderson. They were married Friday Nov. 28 at New Augusta Courthouse. They took a trip to the coast and from there to New Orleans where they will make their home. Everyone wishes them a long and successful life. *The Richton Dispatch,* December 11, 1936, Vol. XXXI, No. 22

Mrs. Mattie Graham Taylor, former resident of Perry County, passed away Sunday morning, Feb. 7, in the Jackson County Hospital at Pascagoula. For several years her health had been bad, so her passing was not unexpected tho it deeply grieved her family and relatives. The deceased, a daughter of Mr. and Mrs. A. P. Graham, of Richton was born in Jones County, Jan. 1, 1903, was married to Chester Taylor, in 1918, and had been a member of the Richton Methodist Church for 16 years. Burial was made Monday afternoon at the Brown cemetery several miles north of Richton. Surviving are her husband and one son, Cecil Taylor, his wife and small daughter, of Pascagoula, her parents, Mr. and Mrs. A. P. Graham, Richton, four sisters, Mesdames John Elkins, Hunter Ivy, Addie Nicholsen and Miss Lillian Graham, of Richton and five brothers, Bob Graham, Hattiesburg, Huey Graham, Greenville, Ira Graham, Union Church and Burs Graham, Richton. *The Richton Dispatch,* February 12, 1937, Vol. XXXI, No. 31

The six months old son of Mr. and Mrs. Doyle Maxie passed away at the Laurel General Hospital in Laurel on last Saturday morning from pneumonia. The body was brought to Richton and interment was made in the cemetery near Brewer School where other members of the Maxie family are buried. Deepest sympathy is extended the bereaved family by their friends and relatives. *The Richton Dispatch,* February 19, 1937, Vol. XXXI, No. 32

On Thursday morning, Feb. 11th, 1937 the death angel claimed for his own Mrs. Rachel L. Draughn, 81, a native of Perry County, a member of the Baptist Church at Indian Springs. She was a kind, loving and social friend to all and one of the truest most consecrated Christians. Survivors are two daughters, Mrs. J. G. Odom, Runnelstown, Mrs. D. G. Morgan, Richton Rt. 3; three sons, Wyatt, Walter and Lawrence Draughn, Richton Rt. 3; two sisters, Mrs. M. L. Batson, Hattiesburg, Mrs. Lizzie Courtney, New Augusta Rt. 1; one brother, A. U. Carter, Hattiesburg Rt. 5 and twenty-two grandchildren.
The Richton Dispatch, February 19, 1937, Vol. XXXI, No.32

Mr. and Mrs. Ben Ruffin are the proud parents of a fine baby girl. The little lady weighed 9 pounds and has been given the name of Jo Nell.
The Richton Dispatch, February 19, 1937, Vol. XXXI, No.32

At eleven o'clock, Wednesday morning Mrs. Eliza West Jordan passed to the Great Beyond following a few days illness from pneumonia. Burial services were held Thursday morning at the Richton Baptist Church with Rev. T. R. Coulter, pastor officiating. Mrs. Jordan who was a member of the Richton Baptist Church was a kind person whom everyone, who knew her, loved very much. She is survived by her husband, Mr. Tom Jordan, her parents, Mr. and Mrs. W. C. West, three sisters and four brothers. Deepest sympathy is being extended the bereaved family by their many friends and elsewhere. *The Richton Dispatch,* February 19, 1937, Vol. XXXI, No.32

Mr. and Mrs. E. E. Burch announce the birth of a son on Monday, March 8 at their home in Runnelstown. The baby has been named Emery Jr. Burch. Congratulations.
The Richton Dispatch, March 12, 1937, Vol. XXXI, No.35

After weeks of suffering Mrs. Cora Myers Black, wife of C. B. Black passed away at the Methodist Hospital in Hattiesburg on Wednesday morning. Everything possible had been done to relieve her but on Monday it seemed her condition grew worse and tho her death was not unexpected it deeply grieves her loved ones and friends, for she was a young woman of exceedingly pleasant personality and to know her was to love her. Funeral services were held in New Augusta on Thursday afternoon at 3 o'clock and burial made in the old Augusta cemetery. Besides her husband she leaves her parents, Mr. and Mrs. I. W. Myers, a brother, Frederick Myers and many other relatives. The Dispatch joins the host of friends in extending deepest sympathy to the bereaved family in this dark hour.
The Richton Dispatch, April 2, 1937, Vol. XXXI, No.38

Funeral services were held at Sandhill Church on last Saturday afternoon for Mrs. Annie Backstrom Walley, wife of Will D. Walley, who passed away at her home on Richton Rt. 3 last Friday. Mrs. Walley was a teacher in the Adult Education program of our county and had many friends who will miss her greatly. She is survived by her husband, five children, her father Mr. K. O. Backstrom, several sisters and brothers and a number of other relatives. Deepest sympathy is extended the bereaved family. *The Richton Dispatch,* April 2, 1937, Vol. XXXI, No.38

Little Charles McLain, the eight year old son of Mr. and Mrs. Jim McLain, of Good Hope community, passed away Tuesday morning as he was being carried to a Laurel hospital for treatment. The child had been ill only since Saturday and while he was very ill his condition was not considered serious until Tuesday. The body was carried to their former home at Piave on Wednesday afternoon where burial was made.
The Richton Dispatch, April 16, 1937, Vol. XXXI, No.40

Funeral services were held Thursday morning for Ammon Edwards, a well-known citizen of this section, at the Odom cemetery, just North of Richton. Mr. Edwards had been in ill health for several years, tho only confined to his bed for the past several weeks. He was living with his daughter, Mrs. Jones in Greene County at the time of his death. He leaves six children, several brothers and sisters to mourn his going.
The Richton Dispatch, April 16, 1937, Vol. XXXI, No.40

Born unto Mr. and Mrs. Dale Hinton, Wednesday, April 21st a fine boy. He has been given the name, Aldon Lamar. Both mother and baby are doing nicely.
The Richton Dispatch, April 23, 1937, Vol. XXXI, No.41

Mr. and Mrs. Austin Odom announce the marriage of their daughter, Louise, to Mr. Warren Hart, of Columbia. The wedding was solemnized on Sunday, May 9, in west Columbia, Rev. Ulmer officiating. The bride is well known here, being the second daughter of Mr. and Mrs. Odom, having graduated from the Richton High School, completing her course in nursing at the U. of T. Hospital in Memphis and for the past year has been employed as County Nurse in Columbia.

The groom is the son of Mr. and Mrs. James Hart, of Sandy Hook, and is a member of the firm, Hart Motor Co., in Columbia. Congratulations are being showered upon the popular young couple by their many friends. They will make Columbia their home.
The Richton Dispatch, May 14, 1937, No. 44, Vol. XXXI

Rev. and Mrs. V. W. Malley announce the birth of a baby girl on May 5 weighing 7 ½ lbs. She has been named Minnie Katherine. *The Richton Dispatch,* May 14, 1937, No. 44, Vol. XXXI

Mr. and Mrs. E. O. Martin are the proud parents of a fine baby daughter who arrived at their home on Wednesday, May 12. Congratulations!
The Richton Dispatch, May 14, 1937, No. 44, Vol. XXXI

Miss Eran Dykes, daughter of Mr. and Mrs. Harvey Dykes, of the Good Hope community, and Floyd Shannon, son of Mr. and Mrs. S. E. Shannon, were married on Sunday, May 16 by Rev. Pruitt, at the Broad Street Methodist Parsonage in Hattiesburg. Their many friends are bestowing Congratulations upon the happy young couple.
The Richton Dispatch, May 21, 1937, No. 45, Vol. XXXI

Announcement is made this week of the marriage of Miss Sarah Cantrell, daughter of Mr. and Mrs. J. B. Cantrell of Richton, to Mr. Dent Ball on April 22. At present, they are located at the Cantrell home. Best wishes of their friends are being extended them.
The Richton Dispatch, May 21, 1937, No. 45, Vol. XXXI

Funeral rites for Mrs. M. L. Newell, 37, who died Sunday in Hattiesburg, were held Monday afternoon at 3:30 o'clock at the Seminary Baptist Church in Perry County. The Rev. Mr. Malley conducted the rites. Pallbearers were: Prent Hinton, J. C. Hinton, Wilson Hinton, R. D. Edwards, Carl Jeffcoats, and Roy Langston. *The Richton Dispatch,* May 28, 1937, No. 46, Vol. XXXI

Wednesday evening at six thirty, Miss Mary Grace Thornton became the wife of George W. Blackledge, Jr., the ceremony being performed by Rev. L. D. Houghton, pastor of the Richton Methodist Church in the parsonage. Only a few intimate friends and members of both families attended. The bride was most attractive in a navy net ensemble trimmed with starched chiffon and using white accessories. The couple left immediately for Hattiesburg and after several days will be at home to their friends in an apartment in the home of Mr. and Mrs. W. D. Mills.
The Richton Dispatch, May 28, 1937, No. 46, Vol. XXXI

Funeral services for Mr. W. P. Vereen, a former resident of this place, were held here Sunday at the Presbyterian Church and interment made in the city cemetery. Mr. Vereen, who was living in Mobile at the time, was found dead in his bed Saturday morning at about 5 o'clock by members of his family. He was apparently in the best of health the night before it was stated. Surviving are his widow, Mrs. Betty Vereen, two daughters, Misses Irene and Betty Ray of Mobile, four sons, Paul of Texas, H. S. Willie, and Ervin of Mobile.
The Richton Dispatch, June 4, 1937, No. 47, Vol. XXXI

Final rites for Mrs. Susie Finley, 66, were scheduled to be held at Good Hope Church Monday. Services were conducted by the Rev. L. H. Turner. Burial was made in Cochran cemetery. Mrs. Finley died at her residence in Richton, Route 2, on Sunday. She leaves: one sister, Ellen Graves, Sumrall; three brothers, G. Clark of Wayne County, Andrew Clark of Louisiana, and Columbus Clark of Seminary; four daughters, Mrs. West of Laurel, May Smith of Vancleave, Ada Edwards of Richton, and Pearl Scarborough, Richton; four sons, Colman Finley of Richton, J. W. Finley of Ovett, Andrew Finley of Louisiana, and Steven Finley of Louisiana.
The Richton Dispatch, June 11, 1937, No. 48, Vol. XXXI

The body of Mr. Wiley M. Edwards, who passed away at his home at Seminary, was brought to Richton on Monday and buried at the Edwards Graveyard in the Good Hope community, Rev. Luther Easterling having charge of the services. Two of the deceased's daughters live in Richton, Mesdames J. H. Riley and Bruce Jefcoats and have the sympathy of their many friends in their bereavement. *The Richton Dispatch,* June 11, 1937, No. 48, Vol. XXXI

Funeral services were held Monday afternoon for Mrs. R. C. Odom who passed away at her home in the Good Hope Community on Sunday. The body was laid to rest in the Edwards Cemetery near the home. Mrs. Odom was the eldest daughter of Mr. and Mrs. W. O. Edwards and is survived by her husband, three small sons, her parents and a number of brothers and sisters and other relatives. *The Richton Dispatch,* June 18, 1937, No. 49, Vol. XXXI

Mr. and Mrs. W. L. Walley of Richton, Rt. 1, on Wednesday, June 16th announced the birth of a six pound son at their home. Mr. Walley was in town on Thursday and in telling about this their fifteenth child said that there was certainly some difference in the weights of their oldest boy and the new one; the young man who is nearing his thirtieth birthday weighs something like 226 pounds and is quite a comparison to the latest arrival in their home.
The Richton Dispatch, June 18, 1937, No. 49, Vol. XXXI

Mr. and Mrs. L. D. Cochran, of Richton announce the marriage of their second daughter, Cora Lee, to Mr. Donald W. Chapman, son of Mr. W. T. Chapman, of Hattiesburg. The rites were solemnized on October 14, 1936 in Laurel. The Rev. Pierce, Pastor of the West Laurel Baptist Church, officiating. They are now at home at 515 Southern Avenue, Hattiesburg.
The Richton Dispatch, June 25, 1937, No. 50, Vol. XXXI

Sunday afternoon, the body of Demaris Draughn Tisdale, wife of Frank Tisdale, was laid to rest in Sunset Cemetery here, Rev. A. C. Parker, Petal, officiating. Mrs. Tisdale, who passed away early Saturday morning at the Methodist Hospital, Hattiesburg, resided in the Dixie Pine community, but as a young woman and for several years after her marriage made her home in Richton, where she was well known. She was the eldest daughter of Mr. and Mrs. Rufe Draughn and is survived by them, her husband, two brothers, S. D. Draughn, of Richton, J. D. Draughn, of Carterville, and seven sisters, Mrs. L. E. Edwards, of Sunrise; Mrs. J. E. Jefferson, of Dixie pine; Willie, Ruth, Doris, India, and Cora Draughn, of Carterville, and a number of other relatives.
The Richton Dispatch, June 25, 1937, No. 50, Vol. XXXI

The five week old infant of Mr. and Mrs. Jim Lott passed away Monday and was buried Tuesday afternoon at Union Church. Rev. W. W. Hill was in charge of funeral services.
The Richton Dispatch, July 2, 1937, No. 51, Vol. XXXI

Mr. and Mrs. W. H. Goodwin announce the marriage of their daughter, Annie Laurie to Mr. Bernard Gibson on Saturday, the nineteenth of June, 1937, Mendenhall. The above announcement will be read with interest in Richton where the bride spent several years of her girlhood while her parents were in charge of the Richton Hotel. Best wishes of their many friends here are being extended the happy young couple.
The Richton Dispatch, July 2, 1937, No. 51, Vol. XXXI

On Sunday morning at 8:30 o'clock, Miss Camille Sumrall and Harold McIlwain were quietly married at the home of the bride's parents, Prof. and Mrs. L. F. Sumrall, Rev. L. D. Haughton performing the impressive single ring ceremony. The bride is the second daughter of Mr. and Mrs. Sumrall and tho having made her home in Richton only a short time has endeared herself to many of the people here. She was graduated from Bay Springs High School and the Jones County Junior College at Ellisville and has a host of friends in South Mississippi who will learn with interest of her marriage. The groom, the youngest son of Mr. and Mrs. J. B. McIlwain, of Richton, grew to young manhood here, graduating from RHS in 1935 and is now connected with the B. M. Stevens Co. *The Richton Dispatch,* July 2, 1937, No. 51, Vol. XXXI

Friday afternoon, the infant daughter of Mr. and Mrs. D. M. Taylor was buried at the family cemetery near the home of Mr. Rance Hinton.
The Richton Dispatch, July 2, 1937, No. 51, Vol. XXXI

Born to Mr. and Mrs. Colon Edwards on June 24, a fine son.
The Richton Dispatch, July 2, 1937, No. 51, Vol. XXXI

On Saturday evening, Miss Kathleen Walley and Mr. Preston Furr were united in marriage in New Augusta. The bride is the only daughter of Mr. and Mrs. Bura Walley and completed her high school work at Richton High School this spring. She was reared in and near Richton and has many friends and relatives here who are showering them with hearty congratulations. The groom is from Brookhaven and is connected with the construction of the highway north of Ovett.
The Richton Dispatch, July 9, 1937, No. 52, Vol. XXXI

A marriage of unusual interest which came as a surprise to their friends, was that of Miss Blanche Watkins, of New Augusta and Mr. Carl Hennig of Biloxi, Saturday afternoon, July 10. The ceremony was performed in Wiggins, Miss., by Rev. Ridgeway, Methodist pastor there. The bride is a daughter of Hon. And Mrs. A. T. L. Watkins. After graduating from New Augusta High School, she took a secretarial course in Hattiesburg, which line of work she has followed up until the time of her marriage. Blanche is a young lady of rare ability and possesses a very striking personality. Her many friends regret that her marriage will take her elsewhere to live. Mr. Hennig, while not well known here, has recently returned from Seattle, Washington, where he was in the Coast Guard. At present he is connected with his father in the Hennig Welding Company, Biloxi, Miss. *The Richton Dispatch,* July 23, 1937, No. 2, Vol. XXXII

A fine boy was born to Mr. and Mrs. Arnold Ball at the Laurel General Hospital on Wednesday, July 22, Congratulations. *The Richton Dispatch,* July 23, 1937, No. 2, Vol. XXXII

A wedding of much interest in New Augusta and surrounding community was that of Supt. H. T. Overby and Miss Donia Mask which was solemnized Sunday afternoon. The living room of the Methodist parsonage had been made a bower of loveliness by the use of ferns and marigolds, green tapers in silver candlesticks cast a soft glow over the entire room where the couple stood for the impressive double ring ceremony performed by Rev. Seth Granberry. Present were the Trustees of the New Augusta School and their wives, Dr. and Mrs. B. T. Robinson and a number of other close friends. The bride, whose home was at Rosehill, has taught in the New Augusta school for several years and Mr. Overby, has served as Superintendent of the school for the past year and is now making plans for a wonderful year in the new building. After a trip of several days on the Gulf Coast and points in Florida, the happy young couple will be at home to their friends in the Teacher's home that has recently been remodeled.
The Richton Dispatch, August 6, 1937, Vol. XXXII, No.4

On Sunday afternoon the spirit of Mr. Rancifer Hinton quietly and peacefully passed into the Great Beyond, after only a short serious illness. Mr. Hinton had been able to come to town up until a few weeks ago and even tho not able to make his usual trips to town with his daughters, he was still able to be about the house until Saturday evening. Mr. Hinton was born on Nov. 18, 1848 and spent practically all of his life at the place where he died. He was a successful farmer and a consistent Christian, being a member of the Baptist faith since boyhood and as long as his health would permit attended church services in Richton. He was the son of William and Eleanor Edwards Hinton, some of the earliest settlers in this part of the state, who came here from Georgia in the early part of the 1800's and his passing marks the last of that immediate family. Funeral services were held at the home of his son, John Hinton, where he had made his home since the burning of the old home nearby, on Monday afternoon at 3 o'clock, Rev. T. R. Coulter officiated and close friends of the family sang some of his favorite hymns of the deceased. Burial was made in the family cemetery near the home. The deceased was the father of sixteen children, twelve of whom survive. These are Burrell, Lancineer, Abner, Ham, and John Hinton all of Richton RFD and Miss Mary Hinton, Mrs. Elizabeth Jones, Mrs. Ida Jones and Mrs. Flora Sherman, of Richton and Richton RFD, Mrs. Ethel Woodward, of Ovett, Mrs. Fannie Woodward, of Hattiesburg, RFD and Mrs. Ollie Mobley, of Bay St. Louis. Deepest sympathy is extended the bereaved family by their many relatives and friends.
The Richton Dispatch, August 6, 1937, Vol. XXXII, No. 4

Born to Mr. and Mrs. Dent Ball, Saturday, July 31st, a son, named Donald Ray Ball.
The Richton Dispatch, August 13, 1937, Vol. XXXII, No.5

Sunday morning Kearney Edwards came into town from his home in the Good Hope Community and went with Carrol Hood, an employee of the Groves Construction Company to carry a day watchman to the job on the highway south of town and as they were returning, the pickup truck in which they were riding overturned landing in water at the side of the road with Kearney pinned underneath. The accident occurred about nine o'clock in the morning just south of Richton about 1½ miles, Hood escaped without injury.

Mr. and Mrs. M. C. Meadows were passing and brought the injured man to town where emergency treatment was given after which he was rushed to Laurel to the hospital where they diagnosed his injury as a broken neck and perhaps others. Here efforts were made to save his life but to no avail. His passing came at 2 o'clock that afternoon with his wife and other relatives at his side. The body was carried to Hattiesburg for preparation and brought on to the family home Sunday night. Burial services were held Monday afternoon amid a large gathering of sorrowing relatives and friends, Rev. V. W. Malley officiating, and interment was made in the Edwards Cemetery a short distance from the home. Surviving are his wife Mrs. Mable Blackledge Edwards, his parents, Mr. and Mrs. J. E. Edwards, three brothers, Claudie, Carl, and Huey and three sisters, Mrs. Theresa Black, of Ellisville and Miss Eva and Thelma Edwards, of Richton Rt. 2. The Dispatch joins the friends and relatives in extending deepest sympathy to the bereaved family. *The Richton Dispatch,* August 13, 1937, Vol. XXXII, No.5

Born to Mr. and Mrs. Sam Walley, a daughter, Thursday, August 19th. Little Mildred is very proud of the fine baby but still can't help wishing it had been a brother. Congratulations. *The Richton Dispatch,* August 20, 1937, Vol. XXXII, No.6

Mr. and Mrs. J. B. Baker are receiving congratulations over the arrival of a fine son at the Methodist hospital in Hattiesburg on Monday. As yet the young man hasn't been named but it is expected he will be named for his maternal grandfather. *The Richton Dispatch,* August 20, 1937, Vol. XXXII, No.6

Funeral services were held at the Frisco Cemetery on last Friday afternoon at three o'clock for Lee K. Buckalew who was killed the previous afternoon by flying stump wood following a discharge of dynamite. Rev. V. W. Malley, Pastor of the Brewer Baptist Church, officiated being assisted by Rev. T. R. Coulter and Rev. Jim A. Smith and interment followed in the family plot in the cemetery. Surviving are his widow, two sons, Furman and J. D., two daughters, Ethel Lee and Arthur Jean, three brothers, Willie, of Long beach, Cal., Arthur, of Jackson, Miss., and Andrew J., of Richton and four sisters, Mrs. Ellis Freeman and Mrs. Clarence Hinton, of Richton, Mrs. A. A. Alpin, of Ovett and Mrs. Thomas Reed, of Brookhaven. Deepest sympathies is being extended the bereaved family by their many friends and neighbors. *The Richton Dispatch,* August 27, 1937, Vol. XXXII, No.7

Funeral services for William Manuel Lucas, eighty, who passed away at Richton Thursday morning, Aug. 26, were held Friday afternoon at the Richton Methodist Church by the Reverend Seth E. Grandberry, pastor of the New Augusta Methodist Church. He is survived by one sister, Mrs. Nancy Ezell, Stonewall; one sister-in-law, Mrs. Victoria Lucas, State line; six nephews and eleven nieces. The choir composed of Rev. V. W. Malley, B. B. Palmer, Griffen Walley, W. D. Cochran, Mrs. Archie Moser, Mrs. P. M. Brown and Miss Lizzie Brown sang "I Need the Every Hour". Pall bearers were P. L. Phelps, Carley Robinson, Roosevelt Walley, Frank Rogers, Charlie Turner and O. H. Newell. Interment was made in the Richton Cemetery with the W. J. Patton Funeral Home of Shubuta in charge. *The Richton Dispatch,* September 3, 1937, Vol. XXXII, No.8

Mr. and Mrs. David Thoms announce the engagement and approaching marriage of their daughter, Mildred Moore, to Mr. James H. Patrick, Jr., of Atlanta, Ga. The wedding will take place October 2, 1937. *The Richton Dispatch,* September 10, 1937, Vol. XXXII, No. 9

Albert (Blacksmith) Newell is the proud father of a 10 lb. baby boy born last Tuesday night. Maybe another Blacksmith in the making.
The Richton Dispatch, September 17, 1937, Vol. XXXII, No.10

Mr. and Mrs. Mack Carter are the proud parents of twin boys. One born on the thirteenth, one on the fourteenth of September. *The Richton Dispatch,* October 1, 1937, Vol. XXXII, No.12

Of much interest to friends throughout Mississippi and Georgia was the wedding at 10 o'clock Saturday morning, October 2, of Miss Mildred Moore Thoms and James Hardin Patrick, Jr. The ceremony was characterized by simple dignity and unusual beauty. The service was performed at the home of the bride's parents, Mr. & Mrs. David Thoms of Richton, Miss., by Rev. J. H. Cothen of Hattiesburg, Miss., a former pastor of the bride, in the presence of the immediate families, relatives, and a few most intimate friends. The setting for the altar was in front of the huge fireplace where ferns and palms were beautifully banked. The mantle was lighted with white tapers held in candle sticks embossed in gold. Adding to the loveliness of the altar were two tall gilded baskets holding white lilies and pompom chrysanthemums, with a profusion of lace fern. Preceding and during the ceremony, a program of nuptial music was given by Miss Dorothy Spikes, violinist, of Richton, accompanied by Mrs. E. E. Lowery, an aunt of the bride, of Sanatorium, Mississippi, Miss Spikes, lovely in black crepe with metallic blouse and wearing a shoulder corsage of yellow, gladiolus, rendered "A Dream". Mrs. Lowery was gowned in brown velvet with a corsage of Talisman roses. Miss Elizabeth Kirkland of Quitman, Mississippi, sang "O Promise Me" and "At Dawning". Miss Kirkland was wearing black crepe and held an old fashioned nosegay of mixed summer flowers. During the impressive ceremony "I Love You Truly" was softly rendered by Miss Spikes. The Bridal party entered to the strains of Mendelssohn's Wedding March. The bride entered on the arm of her father who gave her in marriage. She was wearing a stunning costume of wool and satin in the popular shade of Margot. The jacket of tuxedo effect was trimmed with black Persian lamb. She wore a corsage of orchids, and her accessories were of black. The bride's hat was an alluring high crown poke in black velour, worn with veil thrown over her shoulders. The Maid of Honor, Miss Ann Owens of New Albany, Mississippi, a former college mate of the bride's, was gowned in a soft brown wool crepe costume suit, cape effect, and she wore a shoulder corsage of deep cream roses tied with gold ribbon. Hugh Ogden Thoms, Jr., two-year old cousin of the bride carried the ring in a tiny silver tray. "Little Hugh" was precious in white trousers and navy blue double-breasted coat. He wore a tiny white buttionere. The groom had as his best man Mr. Joel B. Moore of Rolling Fork, Mississippi, a former college mate of his and an uncle of the bride's. Immediately following the ceremony, guests extended best wishes and congratulations to the bride and groom. Mrs. Thoms, mother of the bride, who was wearing a stunning rust crepe with a corsage of yellow chrysanthemums, invited the guests into the dining room to view the gifts. Here they were served punch and Hor D'ourves by Miss Hertha McCormick, assisted by Misses Thompson and Standifer of Hattiesburg. Following this informal reception, Mr. and Mrs. Patrick left immediately for Birmingham and other points. After October 10, they will be at home at College Park, Georgia. *The Richton Dispatch,* October 8, 1937, Vol. XXXII, No. 13

Jake Waits, who up until a few years ago had made his home in Richton and vicinity, passed away at the home of his son, David Waits, in Biloxi, on last Thursday. The body was brought to Richton and buried in the Odom graveyard about noon Friday, Rev. V. W. Malley conducting the services. Mr. Waits, who was about 76 years of age, was the father of Fred Waits and has six other children and a number of relatives and friends to mourn his going.
The Richton Dispatch, October 15, 1937, Vol. XXXII, No.14

Funeral rites for Midd Draughn, 28, who was burned to death Friday night after falling into a pit furnace at a Mobile crate factory, were held Sunday morning at 10 o'clock at the Indian Springs cemetery. Draughn, who had been working in Mobile for several months, was acting as a power house engineer when the accident occurred, Supt. J. R. Henderson reported. He said Draughn was checking steam on the boiler when he fell. The body was not recovered until the boiler flames were extinguished. Survivors are: His parents, Mr. and Mrs. G. W. Draughn, Richton, Route3; four sisters, Rosa and Mattie Draughn of Richton, Mrs. Mattie Henry of Hexton, Colo., and Mrs. E. P. Ramsey of Beaumont, Miss.; six brothers, Carl, Joe and George, all of Richton, Aaron of Merrill, Miss., Alex, Hattiesburg, Route 2, and J. M. Draughn, Hattiesburg.
The Richton Dispatch, October 22, 1937, Vol. XXXII, No. 15

Malcolm D. Fullilove, born in this community fifty-one years ago, departed this life, Sunday, October 17, 1937. He was a licensed Druggist at this place for about 20 years. He married Miss Sarah Young just before the Armistice. In 1918, he enlisted in the medical division at Camp Shelby, went across, and was one day out when they got news of the Armistice, but they continued the oversea journey, and he stayed in France about two months. He was sick about four weeks. It was thought by his physician, at one time that he was convalescing, but about Saturday 16th he relapsed. He was of pioneer stock, his mother Miss Rachel McSwain, who married Charles T. Fullilove, was reared on the ground now composing New Augusta. She was married to Mr. Fullilove at Mobile, more than fifty years ago. They have both been dead about two years. He leaves a widow, Mrs. Sadie (Sarah) Fullilove, and three children, Raybeth and Sarah Edith and one son David, one sister, Mrs. P. J. Thiac, of Bogalusa, La., one nephew, Edwin Cowan, also of Bogalusa, two uncles, C. C. & D. D. Hairston and two aunts Mrs. Florence Hairston and Mrs. A. A. McSwain, of this place. Active pall bearers were Jake Hammett, Carl Myers, Charles Smith, Cecil Hammett and J. C. McDonald. Funeral services were conducted at the family residence, in New Augusta, with rev. Seth Granberry, pastor of the local Methodist church and Rev. W. H. McIntosh of Hattiesburg. Interment was at the Family Cemetery, on the old McSwain Plantation, near Leaf River. He was son-in-law of W. T. Young, New Augusta and brother-in-law to our local Attorney H. D. Young. Brother-in-law to J. N. Thomas, of New Augusta. *The Richton Dispatch,* October 22, 1937, Vol. XXXII, No. 15

Lat Watkins and wife, Willie Price Watkins, have a fine boy born today, their third boy.
The Richton Dispatch, October 29, 1937, Vol. XXXII, No. 16

The many friends and relatives were grieved to learn of the death of Mrs. Sarah Jenkins Myrick on Saturday, October 29. Her passing was sudden having been stricken only a short time before her death at home on Richton Rt. 3. The deceased was 61 years of age, had resided in Perry County all her life, was a member of the M. P. church at Clay Hill, is survived by her husband, James Prentiss Myrick, four daughters, Mrs. Kate Roy, of Grand Bay, Ala., Mrs. Scott Douglas, of Electric Mills, Miss., Mrs. Ethel Pozo, of Port Arthur, Tex. And Miss Ruby Myrick, of Hattiesburg, Miss. and three sons, Riley, of New Orleans, La., and Joe and Zollie, of Richton. There are twenty-two grandchildren and three great grandchildren who with a host of other relatives and friend morn the passing of this splendid woman. Funeral services were held Monday afternoon at 2:30 at Sunset Cemetery in Richton. Rev. Kinsey, of Ovett and Rev. L. D. Haughton, of Richton officiating. Pall bearers were Messers Tip Dobbins, J. T. Carely and Frank Rodgers, of Richton, Jesse Easterling, of Hattiesburg and Irvin Thompson, of Ovett.
The Richton Dispatch, November 5, 1937, Vol. XXXII, No. 17

Announcements have been received by friends of the arrival of little Miss Janice Walley on Wednesday, Nov. 3 at the home of her parents, Mr. and Mrs. Doc Walley in the Good Hope Community. *The Richton Dispatch,* November 5, 1937, Vol. XXXII, No. 17

Final rites for Mrs. Maggie Stevens, 67, wife of B. S. Stevens, were held at 10 a.m. Thursday from the Prospect Baptist church with the Rev. T. R. Coulter, pastor, officiating. Interment was in the Prospect cemetery. Mrs. Stevens died at the family residence in the Prospect community at 1:50 p.m. Tuesday after a short illness. She had resided in this community all of her life and was widely known as a church and community worker. Surviving are her husband, B. S. Stevens; six daughters, Mrs. W. G. Grantham, Richton; Mrs. B. E. Woodward, Ovett; Mrs. E. L. McCardle, Waynesboro; Mrs. L. L. McCardle, Richton; Mrs. T. F. Holliman, Hattiesburg; Mrs. W. O. Hinton, Richton; three sons, J. M. Stevens, Gulfport; B. H. Stevens and C. E. Stevens, both of Richton; three sisters, Mrs. A. E. Heartley and Mrs. P. M. Myrick, both of Richton and Mrs. C. F. Cortney of Florebce; 45 grandchildren and 5 great grandchildren also survive.
The Richton Dispatch, November 26, 1937, Vol. XXXII, No. 20

Last rites for Mrs. Pearlie Foxworth, 37, who died at 11:10 p.m. Sunday enroute to a hospital in Laurel, were held at 10 a.m. Tuesday at Sunset cemetery here. Mrs. Foxworth is survived by her husband, S. A. Foxworth and other relatives.
The Richton Dispatch, November 26, 1937, Vol. XXXII, No. 20

Little Jimmie Holland, the two year old son of Mr. and Mrs. Bill Holland passed away Monday night at a South Mississippi Hospital in Laurel following an attack of diphtheria and other complications. Funeral services were held at the home on Tuesday morning, Rev. T. R. Coulter, officiating and burial took place that afternoon in Sunset Cemetery. Surviving are the parents, grandparents, Mr. and Mrs. J. W. Holland and Mrs. Bruce Jeffcoats and a number of other relatives. The Dispatch joins the other friends of the family in extending sympathy to them in their bereavement. *The Richton Dispatch,* December 17, 1937, Vol. XXXII, No. 23

Funeral services were held at the family home in New Augusta, for L. D. "Dad" Hammett on Thursday, Dec. 16 with Rev. J. H. Cothen, Hattiesburg, Rev. B. B. Blackwelder, of Petal and Rev. Seth Granberry, of New Augusta, having a part in the services. Mr. Hammett, who was an ardent sports fan, was born Nov. 25, 1846 at Greenville, S. C. and moved with his parents, while still a lad to Georgia. He joined Forrest's Calvary at the outbreak of the Civil War and was twice wounded and captured in 1864, serving in a federal prison in Rock Island, Ill. for six months. When he emerged from prison suffering from wounds and illness he was nursed to health by a widow in Illinois and in return for her kindness he worked her farm for her. In 1867 he returned to Georgia and married Miss Cornelia Schiflett. They were the parents of 13 children, only two of which are now living, Mrs. A. A. Campbell, of Heidleburg, and E. H. Hammett, of Hattiesburg. From Georgia, Mr. Hammett went to Talladega, Ala. where his wife died. He then moved to Mississippi and married Miss Sarah Jane Elliot. To this union seven children were born, all of whom are living and are Fred, of Biloxi, French, New Augusta, Jake, L. D. Jr. and Cecil, of New Augusta, Mrs. R. A. McKenzie, Hattiesburg and Mrs. William Ruffin, New Augusta. Being in the sawmill business at Hattiesburg, Bouie, and Bellville, Mr. Hammett made friends as he moved along and later in 1921 he decided to move to New Augusta and enter the mercantile business. He retired from active work about eight years ago. The deceased was stricken with influenza over a week before his death and because of a toxic condition gradually became weaker and soon passed away.
The Richton Dispatch, December 24, 1937, Vol. XXXII, No. 24

A wedding of much interest to Richton and surrounding community is that of Miss Mary Lee Turner and Walter Wallis (Monk) Courtney. The ceremony was performed in the home of Rev. and Mrs. Seth Granberry in New Augusta on December 16, Rev. Granberry officiating. Accompanying the couple were Mr. and Mrs. Buster Blackledge. The bride is the youngest daughter of Mr. and Mrs. Hugh D. Turner, of Hintonville, but has made her home with her sister, Mrs. W. S. Thompson in Richton for the past several months while attending high school. The groom, the youngest son, of Mr. and Mrs. J. W. Courtney has also resided in Richton since childhood. He is a competent electrician and with his wife are soon going to housekeeping. Congratulations and best wishes are being showered on them.
The Richton Dispatch, December 24, 1937, Vol. XXXII, No. 24

Kermit Breland, a truck operator on the S. J. Groves Construction works near Hintonville, was almost instantly killed Thursday just after noon when the truck in which he was hauling dirt stalled as it was being filled. His body was crushed at the chest by the large shovel. He jumped from the truck and fell a short distance from it, dying immediately. He is the son of Mr. and Mrs. B. C. Breland of Good Hope community and was married only Monday to Miss Carey Smith, of Wayne County. Funeral services were held Friday at the family home.
The Richton Dispatch, December 31, 1937, Vol. XXXII, No. 25

On Saturday afternoon, April 15, Miss Jewel McSwain, daughter of Mr. and Mrs. James S. McSwain of New Augusta, became the bride of Mr. J. C. Alexander, son of Mr. and Mrs. R. F. Alexander of Columbia. Rev. Henry A. Wood, pastor of the Petal Methodist Church, officiated at the wedding which took place in Hattiesburg in the presence of only a few friends. The happy young couple are now located in New Augusta, but expect to leave for Columbia in a short time to make their home. Their many friends are wishing for them a most happy and prosperous future. *The Richton Dispatch*, April 21, 1939, Vol. XXXIII, No. 4

News has been received in Richton of the marriage of Miss June Elaine Wamsley, daughter of Mr. and Mrs. E. D. Wamsley, and granddaughter of Mr. and Mrs. J. V. Wamsley, in St. Louis, Mo. on March 15, 1941 to Mr. Leon Blackwell. They are at present located at 3112 Kimberly Ave., St. Louis, Mo. tho they plan to make their home in the West later on. Mr. Blackwell is a great Western Outdoor man. The bride made her home here with her grandparents for several years, attending high school here, and has many friends here who will learn of her marriage with keen interest. *The Richton Dispatch*, March 28, 1941, Vol. XXXV, No. 37

A recent wedding which will be of interest to readers of the Dispatch is that of Miss Mary Emily Garraway, Richton, only daughter of Dr. and Mrs. Charles R. Garraway, Richton, to J. C. Feduccia, of Cleveland. The wedding was quietly solemnized in Pascagoula, Miss. on last Thursday evening, March 20th; Rev. T. J. Carey, officiating. The bride who is an attractive brunette, had made her home in Richton for a number of years, was educated in Laurel and Richton schools, completing her high school work in California, later attending Delta State College in Cleveland and M. S. C. W. at Columbus. Since last fall she had been attending a business college in Mobile. The groom who is a graduate of the University of Mississippi, is a leading young attorney in Cleveland. At present the happy young couple are located in the home of Dr. and Mrs. Perrin at the college campus, and are receiving the best wishes from their numerous friends. *The Richton Dispatch*, March 28, 1941, Vol. XXXV, No. 37

Mr. and Mrs. C. B. Young announce the marriage of their daughter, Jessie Pearl, to J. E. Courtney, of New Augusta, on March 1, 1941, Rev. O. P. Moore officiating. *The Richton Dispatch*, March 28, 1941, Vol. XXXV, No. 37

Mr. and Mrs. L. D. Bush announce the marriage of their daughter, Vida, to J. W. Meadows, of Gulfport. The rites were performed at the home of the bride's parents Sunday afternoon, March 23, with Rev. T. R. Coulter of Richton, officiating. They left immediately for a brief honeymoon to the Gulf Coast. *The Richton Dispatch*, March 28, 1941, Vol. XXXV, No. 37

Born unto Mr. and Mrs. Burns on last week twins, a boy and girl. They have been given the names Virginia and Bernice. Mother and babies are all doing fine. *The Richton Dispatch*, April 4, 1941, Vol. XXXV, No. 38

Miss Mary Ellen Hudson, second daughter of Mr. and Mrs. W. I. Hudson, Richton Rt. 1, was married to Mr. Kenneth Passman, of Hattiesburg, on Sunday evening. The wedding ceremony was performed by Rev. E. A. Kelly in the home of Mr. and Mrs. W. R. Thompson in the presence of a few friends. Following the ceremony the happy young couple left for Hattiesburg to make their home. Mr. Passman is employed in a grocery store there. *The Richton Dispatch*, May 2, 1941, Vol. XXXV, No. 42

Mr. and Mrs. Howard Edwards are the proud parents of a second daughter born on Monday, May 12. Congratulations. *The Richton Dispatch,* May 16, 1941, Vol. XXXV, No. 44

Mr. and Mrs. Hubert Rounsaville announce the birth of a 9 lb. Daughter May 4. She was named Barbara Fay. *The Richton Dispatch,* May 16, 1941, Vol. XXXV, No. 44

On Saturday evening Miss Lessie "Billie" Cooper became the bride of Daniel Stevens at a simple single ring ceremony performed at the home of Rev. and Mrs. T. R. Coulter, Rev. Coulter officiating. The bride, the youngest daughter of Mr. And Mrs. E. H. Cooper, was most attractively gowned in a powder-blue crepe sheer with pink accessories and a corsage of pink carnations. Her sister, Miss Eddie Lee Cooper, who was her only attendant wore pink swiss with corsage of lavender gladiolas. Only a few close friends of the families attended the wedding. Immediately following the ceremony the happy young couple left for a short honeymoon and later will be at home to their friends at the home of the bridegrooms parents near Poplarville. *The Richton Dispatch,* June 6, 1941, Vol. XXXV, No. 47

Miss Josephine Imbragulio, daughter of Mr. And Mrs. Sam Imbragulio of Richton, and William Scott Sibley, Jr., of Crystal Springs, were married on Sunday morning, June eighth, and the Immaculate Conception Church of Laurel, by the Reverend Father T. P. Bowe. Attending the bride was her sister, Miss Helen Imbragulio, of Richton; serving as best man was Mr. Thomas Prince of Camp Blanding, Florida. Immediately after the bridal dinner given by the parents of the bride, the couple left for a short wedding trip, and afterwards visited the home of the parents of the bridegroom. They have returned to Richton, where they will make their home for the present. *The Richton Dispatch,* June 13, 1941, Vol. XXXV, No. 48

Last Saturday afternoon funeral services were held for Luther Nicholson, son of Mr. And Mrs. J. A. Nicholson, at the family home on Richton Rt. 2, and 1:30, Rev. T.R. Coulter assisted by Rev. Clyde McArn in charge. Burial was made in the Brown cemetery in Jones County at 2:30 when military honors were given by a rifle squad from Camp Shelby who were in charge of their captain and sergeant. The bugler for the squad blew taps as the body was lowered into the vault. *The Richton Dispatch,* June 27, 1941, Vol. XXXV, No. 50

Mr. and Mrs. Richard H. Greenwood announce the marriage of their elder daughter, Marie, to Joe Walley on Friday evening at New Augusta, Justice White officiating. Mrs. Walley attended Richton High School and for some time has been employed at Camp Shelby. The groom is manager of Canteen Rt. 12 at Camp Shelby and makes his home at Sandhill. Best wishes of their friends here and elsewhere go with them.
The Richton Dispatch, July 25, 1941, Vol. XXXV, No. 2

Sunday evening Miss V'Allison Brock, daughter of Mrs. V. A. Riley and the later Mr. Silas Brock, was united in marriage to Walter McDaniel, the ceremony being performed by a chaplain at Camp Shelby. The bride is a graduate of Richton High School and has been working at one of the canteens at Camp Shelby for the past several months. Mr. McDaniel, whose home is Stafford Springs, is manager of Canteen No. 15 at Camp Shelby. For the present they will make their home here. *The Richton Dispatch,* July 25, 1941, Vol. XXXV, No. 2

Mr. And Mrs. Ed Turner announce the arrival of a baby daughter on Monday, July 21. The infant weighed 8 ½ pounds at birth. *The Richton Dispatch*, August 1, 1941, Vol. XXXVI, No. 3

Little Odell, the seven year old son of Mr. and Mrs. A. P. Walley passed away at South Miss. Hospital in Laurel on Wednesday evening, following a short illness. The body was laid to rest in a cemetery just east of Richton following a short service conducted by Rev. T. R. Coulter. *The Richton Dispatch*, August 8, 1941, Vol. XXXVI, No. 4

The family circle of the family of Mr. and Mrs. L. R. Hinton was broken last Saturday when their daughter, Miss Eva Grace Hinton, peacefully passed to the Great Beyond. Miss Hinton had been ill for two weeks at the Methodist Hospital in Hattiesburg suffering from a blood disease and all that medical science could do was of no avail. The deceased was 24 years of age, graduated from Hintonville High School, completed a business course at a Hattiesburg Business College and for the past five years had been working for Reliance Mfg. Co. Funeral services were held Sunday afternoon at Seminary Church with Reverends T. R. Coulter and W. L. Yeatman officiating and interment was made in the church cemetery. Surviving are her parents, Mr. and Mrs. L. R. Hinton, of Hintonville; five brothers, Gordon, of Richton; George, of Fort Knox, Ky; Wilson, Ray, and Truman, of Hintonville; and four sisters, Mrs. Earl Hinton, Richton; Miss Delia Hinton, Hattiesburg; Mrs. Baylis Freeman, Albany, Ga; and Mrs. Rush Kittrell, Richton. The Dispatch joins the many friends of the family in extending sympathy to the bereaved family. *The Richton Dispatch*, August 29, 1941, Vol. XXXVI, No. 7

Joe Kennedy, 82, life-long resident of the Mahned community, died at his home there at 10 p. m. Sunday night. Funeral services held at the family residence at 10 a. m. (DST) Tuesday. The Rev. L. N. Blackwelder of Petal, assisted by Dr. W. H. McIntosh, Rev. W. B. Venable and Rev. John Currie, all of Hattiesburg, conducted the services. Interment was in the Old City cemetery, Hattiesburg. Active paybearers were Waldo Story, Little Rock, Ark.; Roy McKenzie, Wilson and Lorenzo Pierce, Nollie Carpenter, and Carl Myers, all of New Augusta. Mr. Kennedy was born and reared at Mahned. He was engaged in the lumber and mercantile business for many years, but was retired at the time of his death. Surviving are his widow, Mrs. J. B. Kennedy; one brother, J. A. Kennedy, New Augusta, and one sister, Mrs. W. E. Griffin, Hattiesburg. *The Richton Dispatch*, September 12, 1941, Vol. XXXVI, No. 9

Funeral services were held Tuesday afternoon at the New Augusta Baptist Church for Mr. James W. Thomas, Reverends O. P. Moore, of New Augusta and J. H. Cothen, of Hattiesburg, officiating. Interment was made in the New Augusta cemetery. Mr. Thomas, who was 64 years of age had been ill for some time and passed away Monday morning at 10 o'clock. The deceased was held in high esteem by all who knew him, as was attested by the large number who paid tribute to him at the final rites. Surviving are his widow and two sons, Jack Thomas, of Grand Bay, Ala. And James, of New Augusta; one grandchild and two sisters also survive. The Dispatch joins the many friends in extending sympathy to the bereaved family. *The Richton Dispatch*, September 19, 1941, Vol. XXXVI, No. 10

A wee daughter was born to Mr. and Mrs. Cooper Ritchie at their home in Beaumont, on Sunday. Mrs. Ritchie was formerly Miss Pearl Davis, daughter of Mrs. T. E. Taylor. *The Ritchton Dispatch*, September 19, 1941, Vol. XXXVI, No. 10

Funeral services were held at the Indian Springs church, in Indian Springs, Monday at 3 p. m. for Mrs. Minnie Lee Hathorn, 63, who died Friday at her home on Route 3, Richton. The Rev. J. H. Cothen officiated. Burial was in the Indian Springs cemetery. Mrs. Hathorn is survived by her husband, J. C. Hathorn; six daughters, and four sons. Miss Ruth Hathorn of Florence, S. C.; Mrs. W. C. McIntire of Florida; Miss Ethel Mae Hathorn of New York City; Mrs. Pearcy E. Haley of Walters, Okla., Miss Catherine Hathorn of Detroit, Mich., and Mrs. John Eadlis of Chicago; Selby Hathorn of Biloxi, J. L. Hathorn of Detroit; Clyde Hathorn of Route 3, Richton; and Claude Hathorn, also of Richton. *The Richton Dispatch*, October 3, 1941, Vol. XXXVI, No. 12

Funeral services were held Tuesday morning at New Augusta Methodist Church for R. B. McSwain, 78, who died Sunday at his home at Old Augusta Rev. H. B. Hilburn officiated. Interment was in the Old Augusta cemetery. Pallbearers were J. A. Fillingane, H. P. Garraway, R. I. Hinton, H. C. Odom, Waldo Storey and Holt Myers. He is survived by his wife, three daughters, five sons and six grandchildren. The daughters are: Miss Naomi McSwain of Oklahoma; and Miss Hazel McSwain and Mrs. Mattie Mae Sanderson, both of Route 3, Richton. Sons are: Robert J. McSwain of Jasper, Fla.; Sam McSwain of South America; Allen McSwain of Meridian; Bruce McSwain of Route 3, Richton, and John Morgan McSwain of St. Petersburg, Fla. *The Richton Dispatch*, October 3, 1941, Vol. XXXVI, No. 12

Mr. and Mrs. Louis Dykes, of Richton Rt. 2, are the proud parents of a dainty baby girl, born Monday. *The Richton Dispatch*, October 3, 1941, Vol. XXXVI, No. 12

The Stork came Tuesday evening and brought Mr. and Mrs. Billbo Prine a fine baby boy.
The Richton Dispatch, October 17, 1941, Vol. XXXVI, No. 14

Mr. and Mrs. L. D. Lowe announce the birth of a fine 9 lb. son on Oct. 8th at a Laurel hospital. She was removed home Sunday and those visiting her Sunday evening were Mrs. Johnnie West, Mrs. Lonnie Odom, Mrs. Joe Hamonds and Mrs. Henry Barnes.
The Richton Dispatch, October 17, 1941, Vol. XXXVI, No. 14

Funeral services were held Tuesday afternoon at the Richton Baptist Church for George R. Dunnam, of Richton Rt. 3, who passed away South Mississippi Infirmary on Monday following a short illness. Mr. Dunnam, who was 70 years of age, had resided near Richton for many years, was well known and held in esteem by the inhabitants of the surrounding community. By trade he was a watchmaker, he was a farmer also. Rev. T. R. Coulter, pastor of the Baptist church, conducted the services and the body was laid to rest in Sunset Cemetery. He is survived by his wife and seven daughters, Mesdames J. H. Broadhead, E. H. Sanford, W. C. Pearce and B. L. Beasley, of Hattiesburg, Rt. 2; Mrs. C. E. Andrews, Richton Rt. 3; Mrs. D. A. Blount, Covington, La; and Mrs. O. J. Boughan, East Point, Ga. Deepest sympathy goes out to the breaved family from their many friends in and near Richton.
The Richton Dispatch, October 24, 1941, Vol. XXXVI, No. 15

Mr. and Mrs. E. H. Sanford are happy to announce the birth of a son, Edward Autry.
The Richton Dispatch, October 31, 1941, Vol. XXXVI, No. 16

A happy romance culminated last Saturday night when Miss Katherine Blackledge, youngest daughter of Mrs. G. W. Blackledge and the late Mr. Blackledge, became the bride of Mr. Prentiss Cartee, son of Mr. and Mrs. T. A. Cartee, of New Augusta Star route. The ceremony was performed by Rev. H. B. Hilbun at the Methodist parsonage in New Augusta in the presence of a few friends. *The Richton Dispatch*, October 31, 1941, Vol. XXXVI, No. 16

Mr. and Mrs. C. T. Turner announce the marriage of their daughter, Joyce, to Mr. James A. Berryhill of Crosby, Miss., on October 25th.
The Richton Dispatch, November 7, 1941, Vol. XXXVI, No. 17

Mr. and Mrs. E. H. Cooper announce the marriage of their daughter, Eddie Lee, to Mr. Dale Gentry, of Richton, the ceremony being performed by Rev. Massey in Laurel on Saturday afternoon, November 1. Accompanying the young couple to Laurel were Mr. and Mrs. Willis Henderson. *The Richton Dispatch,* November 7, 1941, Vol. XXXVI, No. 17

Everyone is in sympathy with Mr. and Mrs. Carol Odom in the loss of their infant girl which passed away Nov. 19th. Mrs. Odom is critically ill in the Laurel Hospital.
The Richton Dispatch, November 28, 1941, Vol. XXXVI, No. 20

Mr. and Mrs. Howard Haynes are the proud parents of a fine son born at the home of Mr. and Mrs. S. E. Swann on Sunday, Dec. 7th. The young man has been given the name of James Howard, and his mother is pleasantly remembered as Miss Edith Swann.
The Richton Dispatch, December 12, 1941, Vol. XXXVI, No. 22

Mr. and Mrs. D. G. Morgan, Route 3, Richton, announce the marriage of their daughter, Arlewaga (Polly) to Harvey W. Runnels, of New Augusta. The rites were solemnized in Prentiss on November 19, 1941. From Prentiss the couple motored to Alexandria, La., for a wedding trip. Mr. and Mrs. Runnels were graduated from Runnelstown High School. Mrs. Runnels attended Jones County Junior College, Ellisville, and was a member of the 1939 graduating class. Later she attended Mississippi Southern College. At present she is a member of the Whitfield Vocational high school faculty at Ovett. Mr. and Mrs. Runnels will make their home in New Augusta where Mr. Runnels is engaged in the mercantile business.
The Richton Dispatch, December 12, 1941, Vol. XXXVI, No. 22

References

American Newspaper Directory by Geo. P. Rowell & Company, Copyright 1885, New York, New York, Library of Congress, www.loc.gov

American Newspaper Directory by Geo. P. Rowell & Company, Copyright 1886, New York, New York, Library of Congress, www.loc.gov

American Newspaper Directory by Geo. P. Rowell & Company, Copyright 1891, New York, New York, Library of Congress, www.loc.gov

American Newspaper Directory by Geo. P. Rowell & Company, Copyright 1897, New York, New York, Library of Congress, www.loc.gov

American Newspaper Directory by Geo. P. Rowell & Company, Copyright 1898, New York, New York, Library of Congress, www.loc.gov

American Citizen, Hattiesburg Miscellaneous Roll #NP-248 MDAH, on microfilm at the University of Southern Mississippi, Hattiesburg, Mississippi

Hattiesburg Dailey Progress, May 24, 1902 thru December 9, 1902 on microfilm at the University of Southern Mississippi, Hattiesburg, Mississippi

Hattiesburg Dailey Progress, December 10, 1902 thru April 30, 1903 on microfilm at the University of Southern Mississippi, Hattiesburg, Mississippi

N. W. Ayer & Son's Newspaper Annual by Frank W. Ayer, Copyright 1906, Philadelphia, Pennsylvania, Library of Congress, www.loc.gov

N. W. Ayer & Son's Newspaper Annual by Frank W. Ayer, Copyright 1918, Philadelphia, Pennsylvania, Library of Congress, www.loc.gov

The Perry County News, April 11, 1912 thru June 30, 1916 on microfilm at the University of Southern Mississippi, Hattiesburg, Mississippi

The Perry County News, July 7, 1916 thru December 21, 1923 on microfilm at the University of Southern Mississippi, Hattiesburg, Mississippi

The Richton Dispatch, April 7, 1914 thru June 24, 1921 on microfilm at the University of Southern Mississippi, Hattiesburg, Mississippi

The Richton Dispatch, July 8, 1921 thru September 10, 1926 on microfilm at the University of Southern Mississippi, Hattiesburg, Mississippi

The Richton Dispatch, December 11, 1931 thru November 6, 1936 on microfilm at the University of Southern Mississippi, Hattiesburg, Mississippi

The Richton Dispatch, November 13, 1936 thru May 23, 1941 on microfilm at the University of Southern Mississippi, Hattiesburg, Mississippi

The Richton Dispatch, May 30, 1941 thru September 15, 1944 on microfilm at the University of Southern Mississippi, Hattiesburg, Mississippi

The Perry County News, Library of Congress, www.chroniclingamerica.loc.gov

The Richton Dispatch, Library of Congress, www.chroniclingamerica.loc.gov

House Resolution 44, 100th anniversary of *The Richton Dispatch*, www.billstatus.ls.ms.us

Surname Index